D1600948

A LIFE OF IMPACT

Newt Becker's Story

A LIFE OF IMPACT

Newt Becker's Story

JOSHUA M. SKLARE

Publisher: Montefiore Press
Editing and project management: Textbook Writers Associates, Inc.
Cover design: Julie Gallagher
Text design and production: Gallagher
Printed in the United States of America

ISBN 978-0-9819265-7-5

The **Montefiore Press** is engaged in the writing, production and distribution of private books. Its sole purpose is to bring to light the stories of exceptional individuals who have made significant contributions in their professional, civic and philanthropic endeavors.

MONTEFIORE PRESS
Specialists in Private Books
www.montefiorepress.com

CONTENTS

FOREWORD

By David Becker

Not many people have the opportunity—and responsibility—of participating in the writing of a book-length biography of their father. I knew my father well. Of course, I had all of the 'normal' experiences of knowing my father, as a father, during my childhood and throughout my life. But I also worked closely with him: First, during my twenties, when he served as a mentor as I founded and ran my own educational business that in many ways was modeled after his, and then many years later, in my fifties, when, eight years before he passed away, I left my faculty position at the University of California, San Francisco, to work closely with him and to run the charitable foundation that he founded.

Yet working on this biography has led me to see him with new eyes—more objective eyes. While most of the first three chapters of the book relate events that took place before I was born or during my early childhood and a close look at those years was new for me, my understanding/feeling about later events has also changed. During my whole adult life, Newt often spoke with excitement about the various innovations that he was making, and challenges that he was facing, at the Becker CPA Review Course and with the many other projects that he was involved with. Both his investments and his philanthropy were intended to change the world, and he was eager to talk about them at family gatherings. So, we did hear about these projects, but since Newt lived in Los Angeles, and I lived in the San Francisco area for most of those years, my impression was usually colored by some event that had just happened, and it was hard to appreciate the 'big picture.' But even more importantly, my impressions were colored by the fact that for my whole life my father had been involved in big things—that was just a natural, ordinary part of my life—and as these projects tended to develop slowly, over many years, with their outcomes always uncertain, it was hard to get overly excited on any given day. Although there were some days, such as when I attended the 1985 inauguration of the world's first solar energy plant, in the Mojave Desert, that would almost certainly never have been built without Newt, or when I participated in a 2003 program in Washington that he developed to bring together about seventy five Jewish Europeans who had the potential to stand up against the anti-Israel propaganda and fury that was raging in their own countries, when I could certainly feel the historic importance of what he was doing.

My thanks to Josh Sklare who, in this book, has tried to tell the whole story, at least the basics of the whole story, from an objective point of view. And by any standard, it is a remarkable story of impact in diverse realms. Josh has based his narrative on extensive interviews and on newspaper and book reporting from the time. My role, aside from interviewee, has been to act as a fact-checker and a sort of "spirit-checker"— to verify that this biography is accurate and captures Newt's spirit and motivation, as best I understand them. For help with the early years, I relied heavily on my mother, Sally Wade, and stepmother, Rochelle Becker. For the later years, I relied on my own understanding of the events of Newt's life, and if something didn't sound quite right, I would work with Josh on the text and/or dig deeper and talk to the right people. After two years of work, this biography is our best effort at an accurate portrayal of the events of Newt's life and of Newt's motivation as he saw it.

One of Newt's legacies, that is intended to last forever, is the Newton and Rochelle Becker Charitable Trust, a charitable foundation that is dedicated to the physical survival and protection of the Jewish people. A large part of the motivation of writing this biography is to capture Newt's story for the future generations of trustees, board members and employees who will be involved with this foundation bearing Newt and Rochelle's names, long after those of us who knew Newt personally are gone. This biography provides insights into Newt's background and concerns, and the approaches he took to address those concerns in his life. I know that he hoped that the best parts of his own life would be a role model for his successors.

Working on the complete story of someone's life is a somewhat unsettling exercise. Over the last two years, we've been through each chapter at least three times. I've also been involved in collecting and sorting photos from Newt's whole life. My experience of delving into Newt's life in his twenties is as recent as my experience of delving into his seventies. The overall effect is to give the feeling that all of Newt's life took place simultaneously, and that it was just a momentary flash in history.

My father lived through an extraordinary epoch in Jewish history that included the Holocaust, the founding of Israel and its survival through many threats to its existence, and the increasing acceptance of Jewish participation in

American life. He was deeply affected by these influences. Some aspects of his own extraordinary life are a reaction to these pivotal events, but always a reaction that involved his own blend of strategic thinking, innovation, risk-taking, a hands-on approach, and perseverance. His life may have been a momentary flash, but it was one that left deep impressions and had tremendous impact.

Many thanks to all who have contributed to this biography. I know that Newt would be proud that his own life is reflected so extensively and so respectfully in these pages. May his memory be a blessing.

David Becker
May 2014

ACKNOWLEDGMENTS

The life of Newton Becker, as multi-dimensional as it was—and, as you will read, he was an accountant, educator, inventor, innovator, entrepreneur, businessman, philanthropist, Zionist, activist, angel investor, and many other things—would require a monumental effort to capture effectively. It necessitated speaking with many people, each of whom was able to shed light on a different aspect of his very rich and diverse life. Interviews were conducted in Northern and Southern California, the Northeast, the Midwest, and by phone to Israel, Indonesia, and many places in between.

In deference to Newt we will begin with his hometown of Cleveland. Norm Diamond and Newt first became friends when they were teenagers and Norm met with me several times, abiding my many questions. I would phone him periodically and he would ask me how the book was coming along. The last time I phoned to do some last-minute fact checking, just several months ago, his daughter-in-law informed me that he had recently passed away.

The Hirsches and the Lashes were also friends of Newt's from their high school years and they spent an evening with me taking me back to the Glenville of their youth. I am deeply appreciative. Likewise to Annabelle Weiss, another Cleveland friend. Eli Becker, Newt's cousin with much knowledge of the Becker family and the firm of Miller Becker, was very generous with his time and added much to this book. Larry Kupps, Newt's nephew, shared much about the character of Newt Becker.

The librarians of the Fairmont Boulevard Temple, the Cuyahoga County Library in Beachmont, Ohio, and the Cleveland Jewish Archives, all made their collections readily available and faithfully answered my many inquiries. Tom Sudow, a family friend, possesses extensive knowledge of Cleveland's history and most especially that of its Jewish community which he was kind enough to share with me.

Very special thanks are due Dr. Norman Meonske, Professor Emeritus of Accounting at Kent State University, instructor of Becker CPA Review Course, and friend and colleague of Newt's. His contributions to the three chapters about Becker CPA were absolutely indispensable and he very graciously spent significant amounts of time with me during my three trips to Cleveland and one trip to Kent, Ohio. I must also thank Becker instructors Frank Prijatel and Nick Sucic, and former Price Waterhouse Managing Partner John O'Brien for all of their help.

In the Chicago area, I would like to thank Tom Vucinic for his contribution to all aspects of the current operations of Becker CPA Review and for sharing with me his own personal interaction with Newt. In the course of my research for this book, I spoke to several dozen current and former Becker students. Though they are not mentioned by name, they shared their experiences with me, both in the course and their desire to become CPAs and thus provided me with a sense of the very real impact of one man, an impact that will continue to loom large many years into the future.

Work on this book saw me travel on several occasions to Washington, DC and I must extend very special thanks to Steve Rosen, who spent most of his career at AIPAC, for his extensive contribution to this book. Yigal Carmon of MEMRI was similarly helpful. Likewise, Jennifer Laszlo-Mizrahi of The Israel Project. In the City of Brotherly Love, I am deeply indebted to Mort Klein of the Zionist Organization of America for sharing his many interactions with Newt and his many insights. In New York City, I spoke with Newt's great-nephews, Rabbis Yirmi and Avraham Berkowitz, who were kind enough to take time from their hectic schedules to meet with me. While in the Big Apple, I also availed myself of the collections of the Center for Jewish History and am appreciative for the help rendered by its staff.

In my own hometown of Boston, I had the privilege of meeting with Andrea Levin of CAMERA who spoke to me of her involvement with Newt. Charles Glick, formerly of Becker CPA Review and proud protégée of Newt's, shared many stories and much information with me. Edmund Case of InterfaithFamily.com, granted me an interview at short notice and I am very grateful to him.

When it came to this book, the Golden State yielded many precious nuggets. In San Francisco, I met with David Becker and his wife, Ann. I am grateful to them for all of their help. You have already read of the critical role David played in this project. To me, it is just another way in which he has continued the legacy of his late father. Dan Becker also has my gratitude for his unique insights.

Southern California proved as fruitful as the Bay Area. I am grateful to Sally Becker Wade for all of her efforts on this project. Likewise Laura and Andy Mintzer and Bradley Gordon. Bryan and Allison Gordon opened their home to me and did much to advance this project. Lois Brodax, Newt's sister-in-law, provided key details. A special word must be said of Rochelle Becker. While Newt's death was completely devastating, she was never deterred from helping me in every way possible. I will remain forever grateful.

Ramin Nadif of Becker CPA Review has my deepest appreciation for spending an afternoon with me and answering many subsequent follow-up questions. Matt Aragachi, formerly of Becker CPA, also has my thanks. David Pollock and George Short, who interacted with Newt as both friend and professional, have my thanks for their unique perspectives.

John Fishel, the former president of the Los Angeles Jewish Federation, and Jay Sanderson, its current head, have my thanks as does Marvin Schotland of the Jewish Community Foundation of Los Angeles. Steve and Rita Emerson, Joyce and Aubrey Chernick, and Irwin Field, fellow philanthropists and friends, were all tremendously helpful. Larry Hochberg, a friend and key philanthropic partner, played a major role in helping me, from encouraging me to pursue this project to providing healthy doses of encouragement and information during its gestation.

Grantees, those who received funding from Newt over the years, were more than just the recipients of his largess. As you will read in the pages ahead, Newt was a mentor and friend to many, providing advice and direction as well as much needed funding. The interviews I conducted with many of them were critical in allowing me to gain an understanding of them. Though I have thanked some of them above, those I mention now were absolutely critical in giving me an accurate picture of Newt Becker.

Deepest thanks to Jonathan Kessler of AIPAC, who explained a good deal about Newt's early years as a lay leader of that organization, and to Ed Beck and Sam Edelman (Scholars for Peace in the Middle East), Boaz Ganor (International Policy

Institute for Counter-Terrorism), Avi Schnurr (Electric Infra-structure Security Council), Anne Bayefsky (Eye on the UN), Gal Luft (Institute for the Analysis of Global Security), Carice Witte (Sino Israel Global Network & Academic Leadership), Yaakov Kirschen ("Dry Bones"), and to all of the other grant-ees who contributed to this work. Nir Boms, whom I originally became acquainted with during the above-mentioned AIPAC policy conference of 2011, has my deepest thanks for sharing so much of his interaction with Newt from their first meeting to the touching tribute he wrote on Newt's passing.

Israelis Raymond Kaempfer, Gil Ephrati, and Orrin Persky, despite time differences and my own lack of knowledge of the world of pharmaceutical research, went out of their way to explain the myriad complications dealing with Newt's biotech investments during our many international calls. I spoke to several people with experience in the solar energy field in gen-eral and with Luz in particular in an effort to educate myself about Newt's involvement in that field and with that very spe-cial company. None were as helpful as Scott Sklar, a major force in the field, who in conversations together brought me back to the exciting and often frustrating early years of Luz.

The transformation from rough manuscript to handsome bound book could not have been accomplished without the work of Laura Glenn, our dedicated copyeditor. Many thanks are due Rose Sklare, our managing editor, who not only plied her considerable talents but provided sage advice throughout the course of this project. Julie Gallagher, who has no creative equal in design and composition, is responsible for the superb good looks of this book.

There is one person yet to thank and that is Newt Becker. Though he did not live to see this project to fruition, he provided me with constant inspiration while writing about his unique life. Countless times I would remark to myself, "Is this man something, or is this man something!" as the enormity of his activities and impact began to sink in. Though everyone with whom I spoke was far better acquainted with Newt than I, I can assure the reader that getting to know him as his biographer has been a true labor of love. To add that the experience of writing about Newt was nothing short of transformative will be evident in the pages ahead. Thank you, Newt!

Joshua M. Sklare
May 2014

A LIFE OF IMPACT

Newt Becker's Story

INTRODUCTION

I have been asked many times over the last several years how I came to be Newt's biographer. It's true that I had done two previous biographies of individuals who were involved in several of the organizations that Newt held leadership roles in, yet his name was not familiar to me until I came across, seemingly by accident, his bio on the website of an organization that I had previously researched. The bio read:

> Newton Becker, a CPA, has a long history of innovative entrepreneurial philanthropy. He has served and continues to serve on numerous boards of directors for organizations including the Jewish Federation Council of Los Angeles, the Jewish Community Foundation of Los Angeles, and the American Jewish Joint Distribution Committee. He has also helped found and fund several other organizations such as the AIPAC Student Program and the campus-based group StandWithUS, two of the most active pro-Israel organizations on U.S. campuses. Mr. Becker is a staunch supporter of Israel and the environment, and in 1980 became founding investor and board chairman of the formerly L.A.-based Luz International. The company was at one time the world's largest solar power plant manufacturer with research and manufacturing facilities in Jerusalem. He is well known among CPAs for the Becker CPA Exam

Review course he founded in 1957. Almost half of all CPAs in the United States are among his former students. He sold this course to DeVry University shortly before his retirement in 1998.

I was certainly intrigued by this most unusual bio, but since I had no immediate connection to Newt and little contact with anyone west of the Mississippi, I went to speak to someone I thought may know Newt. I had met Larry Hochberg several years earlier and he had known four of our previous clients and therefore was very familiar with our work. Given Larry's philanthropic interests and his part-time residency in Southern California, I imagined that he and Newt had crossed paths before. Little did I realize that the two were close friends who had collaborated on important projects as you will hear about later in this book. During my meeting with Larry, he strongly encouraged me to contact Newt, and perhaps feeling I needed a little extra encouragement as I left his offices, he exclaimed, "Newt Becker is the perfect client for you."

So, inspired by such a recommendation, how could I not contact Newt? He was very gracious on the phone and apparently was sold on the idea of having his story told. He was sufficiently impressed by the quality of our firm's work that he agreed to go ahead even before we met. Though I was very pleased, I had the good sense to ask him why he was sold on the idea. His answer was very insightful into his thinking because it demonstrated, as in so many of his endeavors, just how concerned he was with the future. "I want my grandchildren to know why I did what I did in my life." And so they will.

While Newt was very big on communicating by tele-phone and email, I felt it important that we meet in person. Residing in South Florida, I suggested flying across the coun-try to meet him but he had a better idea. "Josh, why don't you meet me at AIPAC?" were his words and immediately I understood he was referring to the annual policy conference of the American Israel Public Affairs Committee held every spring in Washington and I agreed.

Though he was one of 11,000 attendees at the confer-ence, Newt Becker did not simply attend the conference. Rather, he held court there. As people traveled from several continents and all over the U.S. to attend the conference, this was an important annual opportunity to check in with many of his colleagues. Grantees and other philanthropists were eager to bounce ideas off him and feel him out on ini-tiatives. I was later to learn that the one hour he granted me while in DC was precious time given the demands on his schedule.

One thing I learned about my limited time spent with Newt is that he was able to convey a tremendous amount of information in a relatively short period of time. During that hour we discussed so much more than the book project. He gave me his take on the geo-political situation in the Mid-dle East and from there the discussion turned surprisingly enough to nutrition whereby he proceeded to dispense some suggestions on a vitamin regimen. It was during that morn-ing meeting on May 23, 2011 that I came to the conclusion that Newt Becker was like no one else I had ever met and no one else I am likely to ever meet.

We agreed to get together over the summertime to talk more about the project and come up with an interview schedule. In the quiet calm of his Bel Air living room on an especially warm August day, we spent four hours together and this time the conversation free flowed into many areas from the future of solar power, to his early years growing up in Cleveland, to the Six Day War, to Israel Advocacy, to Europe, to Eric Hoffer, back to nutrition, and on and on it went. I was enjoying his company such and enchanted by his rather impressive autodidactism that I did not really want to leave his company, but alas another guest, a major figure in the pro-Israel world, was expected so we said our good-byes and made plans to do some extensive interviewing in several months.

Sadly, that opportunity never materialized. We spoke on the telephone several times and I began preparing a preliminary outline, but the last phone conversation I had with Newt was in October and I sensed that he was growing weaker. I was worried about more than the status of the project; I was worried about Newt. For a time, I could not get a hold of him, and though it was never easy to get him on the telephone, this seemed different. My worst fears were confirmed when I heard sometime in November that he was in the hospital, and then Rochelle Becker called me on January 2nd to inform me of the tragic news that he had passed away.

Their grief notwithstanding, the family decided to forge ahead with this project and so the memoir became a biography. As you heard from David, it was not an easy project, not for him, not for the rest of the family, not for friends and colleagues, and, if truth be told, not for me. His loss was so palpable that it took every ounce of professionalism I could muster as work on the book commenced. Fortunately,

Newt had so many people who cared so deeply about him and his legacy that they would not let up until they had assisted me in every way imaginable. The book that you see before you is a result of that effort.

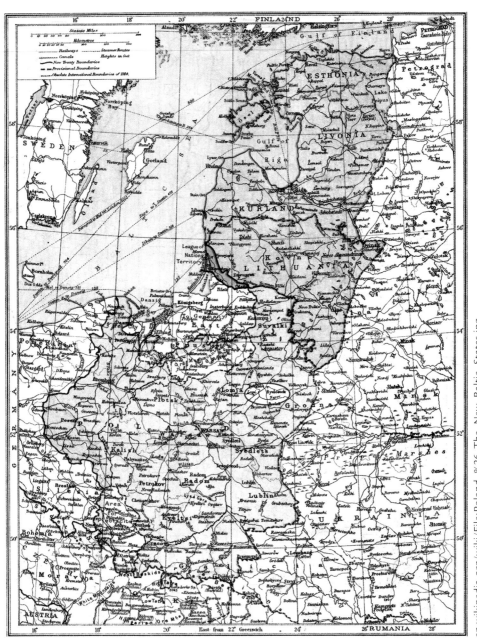

Map of Poland and surrounding countries, published in the 1920 edition of The Peoples Atlas *by London Geographical Institute. The Bialystok (Byelostok) and Lapy (Lapi) region is circled.*

CHAPTER ONE

Beginnings

BORN IN CLEVELAND

Newton D. Becker was born on June 22, 1928, in the city of Cleveland, Ohio. When first asked where his family was from originally, Newt replied, "Bialystok." In fact, Bialystok, the largest city in northeastern Poland, turned out to be the reference point. It was the closest big city to Lapy, a small town about fifteen miles away from where his mother's family, the Rafolofsky family, had resided since the 1830s and quite possibly much earlier.

The town of Lapy may have been only fifteen miles from Bialystok, but in many respects the small town of several thousand people was a world away. The main attraction of Lapy was that the railroad from Warsaw to Moscow, the primary mode of transportation across Poland into Russia, ran through it. Most importantly, the repair facilities were also situated in Lapy, which attracted a large number of workers to the town. Those workers needed to be fed, and that is where the Rafolofsky family business came in.

A Polish shtetl in the 1920s

The family business was a bakery, but it was much more than that. It provided a variety of foodstuffs and other staples like cooking oil, and it was also a purveyor of kosher meat in the town. On the basis of its commercial interests, one can conclude that it must have been among the town's business elite, given the standards of the day. Most Eastern European Jews of their generation, particularly those from smaller cities, were traditionally observant and Jewish life centered around the synagogue. We can infer that the Rafolofskys, although not rabbis like some of their cousins, were lay leaders of the small Jewish community.

Most of what we know about the Rafolofsky family comes from Newt's brother, Phil, who wrote a family history entitled "Zayde Had Dreams—You Have Memories" in 1996, and from a cousin, Eli Becker, who also researched the family history. Newt's mother, Rebecca Rafolofsky, came from a large family. Born in 1890, she was the tenth of twelve siblings. Their names, from oldest to youngest, were Marrum, Max, Gusche, Esther, Hanna, Herschel, Eli, Frieda, Jacob (Jack), Rebecca, Faycha, and Sonia. They were born from 1864 to 1898—a 34 year period! With the exception of three of the siblings—Herschel, who died at age 30 in 1907, and Hanna and Gusche, who were killed during and just after the Holocaust in 1944 and 1945—they would all make their way to the United States along with Newt's grandmother, Anna Rafolofsky, who arrived there late in life in 1925. (Her husband Avraham died in Lapy around 1918, perhaps from the influenza pandemic that we will soon mention.)

Unlike Bialystok and other cities in Poland where Jews actually constituted a majority, Jews were a small minority in Lapy. According to written accounts of the town in the early 1900s, Jews constituted roughly one hundred families, and the Gentile Poles made up approximately three thousand families. One of the major reasons for the large-scale Jewish immigration to the United States beginning in 1880 and lasting until 1921, when Congress passed the "Emergency Quota Act" which severely limited immigration, was the extensive anti-Semitism that prevailed throughout Eastern Europe which included large-scale pogroms in the area. The search for economic opportunity was another motivating factor. However, when in 1905 and 1906 major pogroms took place in nearby Bialystok, people who were thinking about leaving got all the incentive they needed.

A major disaster took place at the end of the First World War: a deteriorating economic situation in Poland and a steady rise of nationalism often translated into episodic outpourings of violent anti-Semitism. The situation was dire and the American government actually got involved. Under the leadership of Henry Morgenthau, the ambassador to the Ottoman

Empire who had been the first to chronicle the murder of Armenians by the Turks, the American authorities received a report from the Jewish Community Council of Bialystok. The report detailed the situation and Morgenthau came to Poland as he did to other places to investigate. Though Newt had not yet been born, and his mother had left in 1917, his grandparents, uncles, aunts, and cousins were exposed to this kind of violence. Surely the news spread to the Beckers in America and one can be reasonably certain that he later heard about it. To give the reader a sense of what was being dealt with by the Jews of Europe well before the rise of Hitler, I quote directly from the report which specifically mentions the Becker hometown of Lapy:

> *Gentlemen,*
> *Already before the evacuation of our town by the Germans—from November, 1918 till February, 1919—the Jewish population of Bialystok was horribly alarmed by the facts of violence that had been committed on Jews by Polish soldiers and gendarmes at Lapy. On this railway station (the 1st in the direction to Warsaw) where the first demarcation line between Poles and the Germans after the armistice passed, the Jewish passengers were most ruthlessly bruised, tortured and robbed of their possessions (to the naked body sometimes!). A real inquisition was there performed and many tens of Jews lost there after terrible sufferings of whippings and blows and moral humiliation their lives, and only the happiest escaped the dreadful death, having endured painful sufferings and material losses.*

In spite of all our protests this barbaric inquisition lasted until its chief—a gendarme-officer—was at last removed from that place, which got a reputation of a "hell" for Jews far and wide.

THE BECKER NAME AND COMING TO AMERICA

There is much speculation about the name change from Rafolofsky to Becker. The standard story is like much of the lore that comes out of Ellis Island. Max Becker, Newt's maternal uncle and the eldest boy, was the first of the 12 siblings to arrive on these shores. Apocryphal as it may be, when asked by the immigration officer what his last name was, he thought they were asking him about his occupation, which was "baker," but came out as "Becker."

This story is contradicted by one which posits that the first relative to come to America was not one of the Rafolofskys, but from the family of Newt's grandmother, Anna Dinovich Rafolofsky (who married into the Rafolofsky family). According to this version of Becker events, her cousin or uncle, whose first name was also Max but who was *not* a baker, was the first one to change his name to Becker, for some unknown reason. He then instructed subsequent kinfolk (the first of whom was Newt's uncle Max Rafolofsky, the baker, who was sponsored by his mother's relative Max) to identify themselves to immigration officials with the last name of "Becker." Word went out to all subsequent family members who would be coming that they should now be known as Beckers. Whatever the exact circumstances and chronology, the end result was that the Rafolofsky family became the Becker family, at least in the New World.

No matter what version of the story one finds most plausible, the end result was the transferring of the family base from Lapy to Cleveland over about a twenty-year period. Though not all the siblings ended up there—the oldest, Marrum, went to Los Angeles, and the youngest, Sonia, went to Detroit—Cleveland became the center of the family, and the place where the Beckers went into the business they knew, the bakery business. Max Becker opened up a very successful bakery that was both a retail and wholesale operation, supplying grocery stores and restaurants. The business became well known for decades by those who grew up in Cleveland.

One of the products they sold in the bakery in Lapy was an early version of soda pop, perhaps better called flavored seltzer. When Eli joined his brother Max in Cleveland, he spearheaded that part of the business which became successful enough that he eventually spun it off into a separate business with a partner, another fellow from Lapy with the last name of Miller. Though they started delivering with a horse and wagon, the operation would in time become very successful and a leading purveyor and bottler of soda pop that would employ hundreds and become known as a regional powerhouse. Uncle Eli, who would eventually change the name of the company to one of the brands, the smartly sounding Cotton Club, had achieved the American Dream and would play an important role in the life and rise of his nephew, Newt. The entrepreneurial dream that would take hold of Newt may have had its antecedents in his exposure to Uncle Eli and the company Miller Becker. Eli was a man known for exacting standards and strong business ethics. Miller Becker, founded in 1902, would span three generations and almost the entire 20th Century before being sold to American Bottling Company in 1998.

Uncle Eli would indeed serve as something of a role model for Newt, and, as we will see in future chapters, Newt was anxious to show that he was cut from the same cloth. Though Eli and Max were both examples of what could be achieved by immigrants, there were other Rafolofsky siblings to be admired as well. One was Newt's Aunt Frieda who operated a successful grocery store in Cleveland with her husband, Abe Leveler. In her later years, she retired to Los Angeles where one of her children lived. She had, like everyone from Lapy, received little in the way of formal education, and while most simply accepted this as part of the old-country status quo, Frieda apparently never did. The encouraging words "It's never too late" were taken to heart by the near nonagenarian and she headed back to school. At the age of ninety she received her high school diploma, cheered on no doubt by her family and her younger classmates as well. It was all quite a story and it caught the attention of the producers of a talk show based in Los Angeles, and so on the night of May 6, 1977, Aunt Frieda appeared on their program. So there sat Aunt Frieda on "The Tonight Show" telling her unique story and trading barbs with the show's host, the legendary Johnny Carson, and her fellow guest, the famous actor, Tony Curtis. Not too shabby, and additional proof, as if needed, that in the Becker family, just as in America itself, anything is possible.

REBECCA AND UNCLE JACK

Newt's mother, Rebecca, came to New York City from Lapy in 1917, at age 26, in order to marry her childhood sweetheart, Phillip Brodax. He had been a teacher in Lapy, and Rebecca had been his student. Brodax was not satisfied with his life as a teacher in a small town in Poland. His ambitions were big, and so were his dreams—so where else do you head but to the Big Apple? Like so many Eastern European Jews, he made his way in New York City's garment trade, ultimately bringing his siblings and his parents to America before sending for Rebecca. Once she arrived, they married and Rebecca soon became pregnant.

Though everything seemed to be going so right, it all went very wrong very quickly. Rebecca's husband was not feeling well one day; it was thought to be nothing serious, just an ordinary cold perhaps. Unfortunately it was more serious than a cold. Within thirty-six hours Rebecca was a widow. Her husband fell victim to what would become known as the Influenza Pandemic of 1918. It was a cataclysm of a magnitude that reminded some of the Medieval scourge known as the Black Death and it was estimated that as many as fifty million people worldwide succumbed to this tragedy. On the heels of World War One, the devastation was extreme.

Rebecca Brodax, as one can well imagine, was in a state of shock and despair. Though her husband's family was in New York, it appears that she was pretty much alone. Her brother, Jack, came to her rescue. Uncle Jack, as he would affectionately become known by all, was another of Rebecca's older brothers, four years older than Rebecca and ninth eldest, whereas Rebecca was the tenth eldest of the twelve siblings. He came from Cleveland to help her with the funeral arrangements and to help ease her suffering. He took her to Detroit—not Cleveland—where she could stay with her sister, Sonia. Then on December 25, 1918, about two months after her husband passed away, Rebecca gave birth to a son, Phillip, who was named for his late father. He would be a great blessing to his family.

Uncle Eli and Uncle Max, big brothers both, and about 10 and 24 years older than 28 year old Rebecca, were the acknowledged leaders of the family, and they were looking for a way for their widowed sister to be able to support herself and her son. Their solution was to have her move to Cleveland, their base of operations, where together with their brother, Jack, she would open a bakery. It was the business that the family knew best, and Uncle Max was already running a sizable operation in the city. The division of labor was fairly straightforward. The two oldest brothers would finance the business, Uncle Jack would manage its day-to-day functions, and Rebecca would work in the front waiting on customers. The additional benefit of the bakery was that it provided living quarters for Rebecca, Jack, and young Phillip. The store's location was Glenville, a neighborhood the family would return to years later.

Uncle Jack was one colorful figure. Sally Becker Wade, Newt's first wife, described him as straight out of a Damon Runyon short story—a Nathan Detroit or a Benny Southstreet—a real character. In a family that valued earnest hard work, though, Uncle Jack marched to the beat of a different drummer. He was probably not quite cut out for the hard work and long hours of running a store, but if there was any doubt about this, the passage of the Volstead Act and the 18th Amendment intervened. For those younger readers out there, we refer to this thirteen-year experiment simply as "Prohibition."

Alcohol may have been prohibited, but people did not stop drinking—not by a long shot. Nature abhors a vacuum, so the speakeasy and the bootlegger became mainstays of the era. While Uncle Jack was a far cry from Al Capone or Abe Bernstein, the leader of Detroit's notorious Purple Gang, he proved to be adept enough in the field that he took a leave of absence from his bakery duties. It turned out to be a permanent leave, and, with his two brothers so busy running their own enterprises, they made the fateful decision to sell the bakery and provide their sister with the proceeds of that sale.

Phillip was still a toddler, and the questions were where to go and what to do? Rebecca had friends from Lapy as well as a cousin who had settled in Chicago, so it was off to the City of Big Shoulders. There she worked in a bakery and raised her son. She stayed for three years; whether she missed her family or other factors intervened, we do not know, but she came back to Cleveland. Meanwhile, Uncle Jack was doing well enough in his new vocation to build an apartment building. According to his nephew, Phil, it contained twenty brand-new units which provided a nice home for the threesome. After watching the great success of his brothers, Eli and Max, Jack had finally made it on his own terms. He owned a building, a very big deal for an immigrant, and it turned out well for his sister, too, at least for a while.

The search had long been brewing for a new husband for Rebecca with the brothers looking for just the right man for their sister and her son. They found a willing suitor in Max Grossman. Rebecca was apparently very beautiful but also very choosy. She had never gotten over the loss of her first husband, who was apparently her only love. Her personality had undergone a genuine metamorphosis after his passing from a happy and outgoing young newlywed to a more introverted and dour widow. Apparently this change stayed with her throughout her long life. For his part, Max Grossman was an immigrant who had served in the artillery during the Great War and had a modest business assembling work crews to clean factories and other commercial buildings.

Newt at age 2 (1930)

From Phil's account, the marriage seemed troubled from the start. Even if you doubt the expression that every cloud has a silver lining, you would be forced to conclude that at least in this case, something very great came from the marriage of Rebecca and Max. It all happened on June 22, 1928, when Rebecca and Max Grossman became the proud parents of their son, Newton Grossman. (Grossman was a last name that Newt kept until changing it to Becker as a young adult, as we'll see in Chapter 2.) Though one could hardly know it at the time, this birth would impact thousands of people, if not millions.

Max Grossman would be involved for only the first few years of his son's life, and, sadly, would play little, if any, role in it. After Rebecca and Max divorced, it appears that Max did try to maintain contact with his son, but the divorce was sufficiently bitter that Newt's mother ended that contact after a short time. Though Newt was surrounded by his mother and Uncle Jack, whom he loved very deeply and who looked out for him, one cannot discount this loss. There was a story Newt told that he did have some brief contact with his father in high school, and there was talk of an automobile that his father would somehow help him purchase, but it never came to fruition.

While his father may not have been much involved in his life, Newt performed a final act of loving-kindness for his biological father. He was already working in accounting at the time. We know of no contact that he had with Max Grossman when the latter passed away; how Newt found out we also do not know, but he took on the responsibility of the burial. One gets the feeling that Max Grossman had a difficult life. Given the story, it is assumed that his father never remarried or had any other family. His only real impact in the world may have been fathering Newt, and while his son rarely spoke of his father, neither did he deny him. Perhaps it should also be mentioned that this final act of kindness was typical of Newt; he did the right thing, the responsible thing, no matter the range of emotions that surely he must have felt at the moment. It was part of a greater pattern of behavior that we will see repeated throughout his life.

"WHAT ARE THE RICH JEWS DOING TO PROTECT US?"

Though he was only a boy when the Nazis came to power in 1933, and merely a teenager when the war began six years later, the Holocaust and the inaction of the civilized world to prevent the destruction of European Jewry played a pivotal role in Newt's life. While the Nazi rise to power and the anti-Semitism that would precede the Final Solution would be far from the consciousness of many Americans including American Jews, Newt was very sensitive to it. There were large protests in America including those held in Madison Square Garden. In Cleveland, the Jewish War Veterans took to the streets soon after the Nazis came into power. There was a Jewish boycott, one in which Rabbi Abba Hillel Silver, whom you will meet shortly, played a major role.

With the exception of Rabbi Silver and a few others, the Jewish leaders of that generation were not in the mold of Newton Becker's activist style, thus many were afraid to assert themselves. There was a good reason for that, or so they must have thought. The Thirties were radically different times from our own, with Father Charles Coughlin, an anti-Semitic Catholic priest from Royal Oak, Michigan, spewing invectives against the Jews on the radio airwaves. He found a willing audience, as did the German American Bund and the Silver Shirts, Nazi sympathizers both, marching, holding rallies, and otherwise intimidating Jews. It was a scary time to be Jewish, even in America, and with the period's increased anti-Semitism came a form of reactionary isolationism that tried to move America from involving itself in the affairs of Europe in general, and Germany in particular.

Newt's mother Rebecca, Newt at age 10,
and Newt's brother Phil (1938)

There was also the feeling among certain Jewish leaders during this period that it was best to follow the proverb, "This too shall pass." It was something that Newt would also hear plenty of after 9/11, and perhaps his resistance to this notion in the first decade of the 21st Century came straight out of his exposure to the 1930s. It was a very bad decade for the Jewish people, and, in early November of 1938, things got even worse. Though he was thousands of miles away, protected by an ocean and presumably the U.S. government, the two-day period of nonstop pogroms known collectively as the Night of Broken Glass, or Kristallnacht, was felt very strongly by the young Newt Becker. David Becker, Newt's son and successor in running the Newton and Rochelle Becker Charitable Trust, while eulogizing his father, describes the impact.

"Newt talked about the night of Kristallnacht, which as most of you know, occurred on November 9th and 10th, 1938 when Nazi stormtroopers and civilians went on a rampage in Germany and damaged or destroyed hundreds of synagogues, seven thousand Jewish-owned businesses, and killed ninety-one Jews—with the German police standing aside. Newt was ten-and-a-half years old. He remembers listening to the radio and being terrified. Apparently, his whole neighborhood was afraid of what we today would call "copycat" violence. A group of older teenage boys carrying baseball bats went to the edge of their neighborhood to protect it.

At ten years old, Newt was too young to stand guard with the older boys, but old enough to know what was going on. He understood that a handful of boys with baseball bats was not very good protection from the kind of violence he was hearing about on the radio, and he was scared. It was at that point that he remembers asking the question that would later guide his life: "What are the rich Jews doing to protect us?"

Newt did have one uncle who was a successful business owner—so Newt knew that there were some wealthy Jews. Newt decided if he were ever "rich" like his uncle, he would do his part to protect the Jewish people.

It was a promise he would keep.

Some years later, the murders of the Holocaust also struck close to home. We heard earlier about the loss of two of his

Newt (3rd row, second from left) and class at Patrick Henry Junior High School

mother's siblings during the war. Newt's Aunt Hanna had stayed in Lapy with her husband, and, during the Holocaust, they were murdered by the Nazis. Newt's Uncle Gusche also stayed in Lapy and inherited most of his parents' property. During World War Two, Gusche was protected and hidden by Christian friends, but when the war was over and he felt free to walk the streets of Lapy, he, at 76 years old, was killed by a roving band of hoodlums who were still intent on killing Jews. Apparently, this kind of tragedy was not unusual as one can find documentation of another Lapy family who lost two of its members to a similar fate shortly after the war.

Newt must have known that had his mother not taken the fortunate step of coming to America decades earlier, the same fate that befell six million Jews would have been his. What's more, as a student of history, Newt was aware that if Rommel had not been stopped in El Alamein, and if Hitler had not been defeated in Europe, then the Jews of Palestine and America would have indeed been in peril. Again, it is worth bearing in mind when we hear about his concerns after 9/11 later in this book.

THE INFLUENCE OF JEWISH CLEVELAND

The goal of this chapter is to examine and understand the forces that shaped the formative years of Newton D. Becker. One of the major questions that arises from an examination of his life is where he obtained his tremendous sense of responsibility for giving, and his great desire to play a leading role in Jewish philanthropy. Part of the answer may lie in the place where he was raised, the city of Cleveland, Ohio. The influence of the city, whether in his childhood or early adulthood, was especially felt in regard to the city's Jewish community and leadership. This was pointed out by John Fishel, former top executive of the Los Angeles Federation, who, like Newt, was a native of Cleveland.

While Newt may have found the city's wealthy Jews to be lacking in their ability effectively to help their brethren in Nazi Germany, it seems clear that he was impressed by their ability to tend to the social welfare of the local community. Cleveland does have the advantage of a goodly number of very wealthy families with names like Ratner, Mandel, and Stone. Despite having only the twelfth largest population of Jews in U.S. cities, the top federation executive in Cleveland is often the highest paid, exceeding cities such as New York, Los Angeles, Chicago, and Philadelphia. The pride taken, not just by Cleveland's wealthy but by its entire Jewish community, in its ability to raise large sums both at home and for Palestine—and later Israel—is something that Newt must have internalized. It helped facilitate the way he viewed his own responsibilities as he climbed the professional and economic ladder.

Cleveland was a hotbed of Zionist activity in Newt's formative years. Rabbi Abba Hillel Silver, a preeminent rabbinic leader, along with Justice Louis Brandeis, were Zionism's most prominent spokesmen. At one time or another, each of them led the Zionist Organization of America, an organization which, in later years, Newt would strongly support, and Rabbi Silver made a passionate plea for Jewish statehood before the U.N. General Assembly.

To give the reader a sense of what a Clevelander of Newt's era would have been exposed to, Rabbi Silver expressed his view of Jewish life and a Jewish state this way: "The upbuilding of a Jewish national home in Palestine is one of the great, urgent and historically inescapable tasks of Jewry. The

*Newt at about 16
(~1944)*

upbuilding of Jewish religious life in America and elsewhere throughout the world, inclusive of Israel, is another. One is no substitute for the other. One is not opposed to the other." You will no doubt think throughout this book as we discuss Newton Becker, that the following applies equally to Abba Hillel Silver: "They ain't making them like that anymore." He influenced Cleveland and the world, and it is hard to believe that he did not have some impact on a young Newt Becker.

Though he would eventually join a reform congregation in Cleveland, and later in Los Angeles, at that time Newt attended the preeminent conservative congregation, the Park

Synagogue, led by another rabbinic giant of the era, Rabbi Armond Cohen. Rabbi Cohen served the congregation for seventy-three years, a tenure which should have landed him in the Guinness Book of World Records. Newt went to the synagogue's teenage program and his confirmation class picture hangs there to this day. Newt attended the prominent congregation not because his mother or Uncle Jack were members. As you will soon see, they were barely getting by in those difficult years and could never have dreamed of affording such a luxury. This probably explains why Newt never had a Bar Mitzvah. When Newt did participate in the life of Park Synagogue, it was as a consequence of being the nephew of one of its distinguished members, Newt's uncle, Eli Becker.

TOUGH TIMES

One of the factors that played into all of the terrible events of the 1930s was the Economic Depression, which began with the Stock Market Crash of 1929. This impact was felt in Newt's boyhood when Uncle Jack lost his treasured apartment building to the bank in 1930 because so many of his tenants were out of work and could not afford to pay rent. Though this was very common and ruined many landlords of much larger buildings, for Uncle Jack this loss was a good deal more than just financial. It was a loss of pride, a loss of status, and the loss of a home. He had beseeched some family members to help him make the payments, but, due to a number of factors including their own troubles during the Depression, this help never materialized. Uncle Jack was embittered. He was still doing well enough with liquor sales to move the family to a very nice duplex in Cleveland Heights. Things were going to get very sober, however, with the 1932 election of Franklin D. Roosevelt, who had made a campaign promise to end Prohibition, which he did in December 1933.

"Happy Days Are Here Again" was the theme song of FDR's campaign, but it was not a refrain sung by those in Uncle Jack's line of work. He was essentially put out of business. Though he did manage to make some money in different ventures in his life, it was mostly a colossal struggle for him to make a living. This struggle was felt by Rebecca, who took on work as a seamstress, as well as by Phillip and Newton. They spent a lot of time moving from place to place while Uncle Jack struggled to come up with money for rent. Whatever status and luxuries he had enjoyed were now fully gone. He was bitter, but he pushed on largely for the sake of his two nephews.

Jack did prove to be creative in finding one place after another; somewhere he had an opportunity to own, but he never could find the necessary funds. The foursome finally caught a break sometime around 1937. Phil had just finished high school when Uncle Eli invited them to move into a five-room apartment of a two-flat that he had recently acquired. It was on Parkwood Drive in Glenville, and was right across the street from Glenville High School.

In addition to providing them with an apartment and allowing Newt to use his membership at the synagogue, Uncle Eli provided help in other ways. Things became so bad for Uncle Jack that one winter—and Cleveland winters were brutal as the biting wind off Lake Erie went right through you— he could not afford to buy Newt a desperately needed winter coat. With no other option, he went to Uncle Eli who happily allowed him to charge it to his account at one of the city's best department stores. After graduating from high school, Phil would work at Miller Becker during those years when having any form of employment was much valued.

Winters were tough in other ways as well. Keeping one's body warm when outside was one thing. Keeping it warm while inside was sometimes equally challenging. Their place was heated with coal, but the times were so trying that Uncle Jack could not afford to buy it. Uncle Max allowed his brother, together with Phil and Newt, to come down to the bakery and take coal from the large shipments that arrived every day to heat their substantial ovens. In addition to taking their coal, they were also allowed to load up on two-day-old bread and pastries, which, with the right toasting, heating, and subsequent dunking, must have tasted good and may have been the source of Newt's famous sweet tooth. Or perhaps it was the sweet soda pop including their famous Cotton Club ginger ale that Uncle Eli provided the family.

Newt also got some exposure to what we might call the good life, as he would visit Uncle Eli's cottage in the summer, located in Ashtabula, Ohio. Together with his brother and cousins, he could swim to his heart's content and enjoy the festive picnics his aunt prepared. It was a testament to the success of Miller Becker that not only did they have a nice cottage but an extra lot where the kids would play all manner of games including croquet.

Help was also extended by Newt's Aunt Frieda, the famous *Tonight Show* star whom we spoke of earlier, and her husband, Uncle Abe. They owned a grocery store and helped the family out with some staples, especially canned goods. Phil points out that due to their family's network, their household never suffered as others did. But all of this assistance was never forgotten, and what we see from the life of Newt Becker is that he paid it forward, helping not only relatives in any way he could, but anyone who came into his life. The man knew what it was like to be dependent on others.

Phil and Newt from their earliest years also contributed to the household income. As many are no doubt aware, whether employees of Becker CPA or employees of any of the number of charities he supported, Newt had a strong affinity for work. Again, it was a question of necessity being the mother of invention as he sought any legal way to bring in a dollar. Bryan Gordon, Newt's son, told me that during the summers Newt would buy a box of ice creams for 50¢, and with a markup of four times he would sell the entire basket for $2.00, his only other cost being dry ice to keep them frozen. It must have taken a lot of effort on his bicycle to make that $1.50, but it was big money in those days. An early entrepreneurial venture, it must have made a big impression on the young Newt. What did young Newt do during the winter? There was no shortage of snow in Cleveland, but, rather than spend his time frolicking in it, building a snowman, or maybe going sledding, he was too busy making money with a shovel.

GLENVILLE AND GLENVILLE HIGH SCHOOL

The move to Parkwood Drive in Glenville helped bring some stability to Newt's formative years. While he spent much of his childhood going from apartment to apartment because of the Depression-era struggles of Uncle Jack, 801 Parkwood Drive proved something of an oasis in those unsettling times. Perhaps best of all, it allowed Newt the opportunity to attend Glenville schools, both its middle school and its famed senior high school, Glenville High.

Glenville was in the 1920s, '30s and '40s a working-class Jewish neighborhood on par with Chicago's Lawndale or Brooklyn's Brownsville. Like all such ethnic enclaves in urban America, it had its own distinct rhythm and was a model of how primarily Eastern European immigrants were adapting to a new life. The beat and the eats of Glenville are beautifully captured by Sidney Vincent, a coauthor of *Merging Traditions, Jewish Life in Cleveland*. As is the case with any neighborhood, the boundaries are critical, as Vincent conveys:

> *It was only north of Superior Avenue (along 105th street) that the Jewish neighborhood really came into its own. Almost every block from Superior to St. Clair had its own shul (synagogue) and its own kosher market—fruit and vegetable markets. All of them were meeting places where Jewish events were discussed and where the shape of the day and the week were permeated with the rhythm of Jewish life, reflected not only in the almost total closing down of business on the Jewish holidays, but also in the shared experience of shopping and dating and discussing in an atmosphere that took Jewish concerns and Yiddishkeit for granted. At class reunions nostalgic memories are still traded—of waiting for "my next" on Saturday night at the jammed meat market, or buying corned beef at Solomon's on Massie Avenue, or smelling the newly baked rye and pumpernickel in any of the bakeries clustered around Earle and Gooding Avenues.*

Among his classmates Newt was known affectionately as "Newty." In his high school yearbook, his activities were listed as Olympiad, Radio, and Class Entertainment Committee. It appears that nearly everyone in the class of 1946 participated in school activities. From the looks of the many class photos, there is no sense of the disaffected adolescent anywhere. These students seem serious, focused, and loyal. These were, after all, serious times. A world war had raged for three of their four high school years. When they first entered the hallowed halls of Glenville High School as freshman, it is likely that there were outgoing seniors and some juniors who would serve in the conflict. Some would come back to Glenville High School to show their former classmates their medals and their mettle. Some never made it back to Glenville, having spent their last minutes on earth on the battlefields of Europe or the Pacific Islands. Their names are listed in class bulletins at Glenville High School just as they must have been in high schools throughout the country. It was a sobering message for the class of 1946.

In the course of the research for this biography, a friend of Newt's asked if Newt was a particularly outstanding student in high school, thinking that with his ingenious mind, he must have been. This author queried several of his classmates from Glenville to find the answer to that question and to ascertain if there had been any hint of the great success that would follow years later. Like many other successful types, it appears that he did not provide an inkling of what was to come. My sense is that Newt was a good student but not a great one and that there was no premonition as to what would follow. But Newt was different from many who grew up in such ethnic neighborhoods who, after leaving their hometown high school, show little interest in their alma mater. Not only did Newt take great interest, but he happily paid for many class reunions including a momentous sixty-fifth held in Cleveland in 2011, the last year of his life. His classmates were naturally enough very proud of the man he had become; his stature and his largess were well appreciated, not just for the evening reunion but for a brunch he sponsored the following day. But for all of his success, he did not lord it over people, and he did not think it earned him special privileges. Newt had traveled to that last reunion by himself and thought it would be nice if his good Cleveland buddy, Norm Diamond, joined him despite the fact that Norm was not a Glenville grad. He called Art Hirsch, one of the organizers of the event, to ask permission to bring Norm along; of course, Art was only too happy to extend an invitation. Another person who was underwriting such an event would have just informed Art that he was bringing a friend. After all, most people would think to themselves, "I am paying for this thing, so I can do what I like." But that was just not Newt. It is no wonder his friends from Glenville felt so comfortable with him. He really was the same guy they knew from high school, just presently equipped with a healthier checkbook.

A certain type of high school teacher or guidance counselor seeks to impart the sense that armed with an education and the right plan, you can go as far as your ambition takes you. In America, that has been a common enough theme. For a sixteen- or a seventeen-year-old in Glenville, those optimistic sentiments may have also been reinforced by the aspirations of immigrant parents. For the Glenville class of 1946, they could point to some of the prominent graduates of the past for inspiration.

A few of the notable alums from Glenville included Gordon Allport, renowned psychologist, Harvard professor, president of the American Psychological Association, and a personality who was a leading authority on personality. There was Al Lerner, a fixture of the Big Band Era, and famous pianist, composer, and conductor. Two students with big imaginations, Jerry Siegel and Joe Shuster, created the comic book character known as Superman while attending Glenville High School. They based the character of Clark Kent on one of their classmates, Wilson Hirschfeld, an aspiring journalist who would go on to become managing editor of the *Cleveland Plains Dealer*. There was Hal Levovitz, legendary sports writer; and Roy Solomonoff, a physicist and early pioneer of Artificial Intelligence. Jerome Lawrence was a Glenville alum who became a playwright and wrote *Inherit the Wind*. One of the poorest of kids to attend Glenville was Howard Metzenbaum, who became very, very rich and wielded enormous power as a U.S. senator. But for all these luminaries, the most famous student ever to grace Glenville High was Benjamin Friedman, known as Benny, who, after leading the Glenville Gridiron to many victories, became an All-American quarterback at Michigan and revolutionized professional football during his career. To the students of Glenville in football-crazy Ohio, he was a beloved and admired figure. He enjoyed similar status throughout the American Jewish community.

It is worth mentioning that, with the exception of Allport, all were Jewish, and the message to a young Newton Becker was that in America anything is possible. One senses a can-do spirit in the Glenville of those years, and Newt would follow in the footsteps of some of the grads we have mentioned. For most of those like Metzenbaum and Friedman, the key to success was college, and for Newt Becker there was never any doubt that he was headed there upon graduation from Glenville High School in 1946; Kent State awaited.

CHAPTER TWO

Kent State, Dachau, and Price Waterhouse

FROM NEWTON N. GROSSMAN TO NEWTON D. BECKER

The transition from Newton N. Grossman to Newton D. Becker occurred sometime between his graduation from Glenville High School in 1946 and 1951, when some correspondence from Germany was signed Newton Becker. It was not possible to determine the exact date, but it is likely that he changed his name either at the beginning of his college years or perhaps before his induction into the U.S. Army. Only those who knew him intimately or for many years knew of his original last name. Why did he change his name?

We spoke in the first chapter about Newt's relationship with his biological father, Max Grossman, who played a very small role in Newt's life. Newt was raised by his mother and her brother, his Uncle Jack Becker, who, like all of his brothers and sisters took the name Becker at Ellis Island. Newt had strong relationships with many of his mother's family members, such as his Uncle Eli Becker. Whether he would have changed his name or not, it seems clear that he would have thought of himself as a member of the Becker family, so that the legal formality of becoming a Becker was partly a reflection of his internal mindset.

Then there is the legacy of Newton D. Baker (1871–1937) to add to the equation. For those readers unfamiliar with the powerhouse political figure, Baker was a distinguished public servant who served as mayor of Cleveland from 1912 to 1915. He had long known Woodrow Wilson, dating back to Wilson's days in academia. When the president was preparing to lead the country into an intervention into what was seen as a European war, he needed an exceptional figure to head the War Department. President Wilson tapped Baker as his secretary of war, who served in that capacity between 1916 and 1921.

Baker was no ordinary politician. His gravitas and his powerful feel for oratory can be noted in a speech given at the Democratic National Convention in 1924. Just five months removed from the death of his mentor, Woodrow Wilson, Baker urged the convention to follow the lead of the late president and not succumb to the temptation of isolationism, a movement that was to define the country politically until the attack on Pearl Harbor.

Baker, in addition to his political activities, was also an outstanding legal practitioner who argued cases before the U.S. Supreme Court. He was mentioned as a candidate for both president and vice president during the 1920s and early 1930s. As a native of Northeast Ohio, Newt would have been inculcated from an early age with a high regard for one of Cleveland's favorite sons. It has been mentioned to me that Newt, as is the case with many who have the combined attributes of ambition and idealism, had some thoughts of giving politics a try in his early years, and that may have led to his attraction to Baker. Though he declined to ever make a run for public office—and as you will see throughout the course of this book, he often played a quiet, behind-the-scene role—becoming Newton D. Becker would accomplish two things: most importantly, it would connect Newt with his mother's family, but, in addition, by taking Newton Baker's middle initial (which was short for Diehl, probably a family name), it would link him with that political icon and his hallmark attributes: honesty and integrity.

Although his identification with the Becker family and the resonance of the Newton D. Baker name were significant, perhaps the most important reason for his name change was that Grossman sounded too Jewish. Newt was well aware of the anti-Semitism of his day and often spoke of it to his own children who grew up in a different era when overt anti-Semitism was more of a fringe phenomenon, at least in the circles that they traveled in. Although he rarely spoke about the name change, he did tell his son David, that it was related to anti-Semitism. This was not a question of rejecting his identity as a Jew: it is clear that his Jewish identity was never shaken.

Instead, it seems that it was a pragmatic move by an ambitious young man who felt he could go farther without having a name that announced to each new acquaintance that he was Jewish.

KENT STATE

The college campuses in 1946 were filled with high school graduates like Newt Becker. They were also inhabited by a group of men in their early twenties, whose life experience belied their young age: World War II veterans, many of whom had seen significant combat and experienced horrific sights in Europe and the Far East, and now were attending college on the GI Bill. It was in this immediate postwar period that college attendance reached unprecedented levels. College was no longer strictly the province of the upper classes. It was more widely available to middle- and even working-class kids like Newt, and he chose to attend Kent State University, located roughly an hour away from his Cleveland home.

We know very little about Newt's college years. He was a thoroughly practical young man and presumably that played into his decision to study accounting. At Newt's 80th birthday party, Newt's son, David, told the true story of Newt's first year at Kent. He took three courses: Accounting, Anthropology, and Art. He received a C in Art, a B in Anthropology, and an A in Accounting—and the rest is history. David joked that had Newt started reading at the end of the course catalogue (zoology for instance), who knows where he'd have ended up.

Were there professors who had influenced Newt during his years at Kent? We know from Norm Meonske, a longtime friend and Becker instructor, that Newt felt that two professors

Newt (about 1950)

had been particularly helpful and encouraging to him, and years later he donated sums of money in their honor as was typical of a man who never forgot the help that others rendered him.

To support himself, Newt held a variety of jobs. Though, unlike his brother, it appears he did not work in the bottling plant of Miller Becker. At various times he was a Fuller Brush man (selling brushes door-to-door), sold shoes, and performed sundry jobs, all of which led him to be able to support himself and pay for his college education. It appears that he received no outside assistance, which probably aided greatly in his sense of independence and the importance of paying his own way.

It was not all hard work at Kent. Newt was a member of AEPi, an international Jewish fraternity with chapters in most of the major public and private universities. Newt remembered the frat fondly. Though it does not appear to have played a major role in his life, and he does not seem to have been particularly active in the national chapter after graduation, AEPi posted this message shortly after his passing:

> *"Philanthropist and Alpha Epsilon Pi Brother Newton Becker (Kent State 1952) entered chapter eternal on January 2, 2012."*

This was followed by a link to his obituary in the *Cleveland Plains Dealer*. They also list him as one of its famous brothers, alongside fellow Kent Stater and CY Young Award Winner Steve Stone, as well as other national notables like Sandy Weil and Gene Wilder.

PFC NEWTON BECKER

The National Guard has its roots in the militias of colonial America but was greatly expanded due to the National Defense of Act of 1916, spearhead by guess who: Newton D. Baker. The modern-day draft was also an invention of one Newton D. Baker, and sometime after the draft was reinstated in 1948 (the country drafted only around 20,000 men that year), Newton D. Becker volunteered and joined the Ohio National Guard. In early 1950, when Newt was just months

PFC Becker

away from graduation, he was called to active duty in the U.S. Army. Events more than half a world away in the Korean peninsula had intervened, and with the police action known as the Korean War underway, fresh troops were a necessity.

Newt had been made a company clerk during his time in the Guard. No doubt his accounting background and organizational skills led to this appointment. He also had another skill that likely was central to his being chosen for the assignment.

Newt and Norm Diamond at Rhein-Main Air Base (1951);
Newt and friend (1952); Newt (1951)

Unlike most men of his era, Newt Becker knew how to type. While most members of the Guard were sent off to combat in Korea, word came down from headquarters that a unit in Germany was in desperate need of a company clerk, so within a short time of being called up, it was off to Rhein-Main Air Base, near Frankfurt.

While American troops originally entered Germany as part of an occupying force and remained there to de-Nazify the country, there were other reasons for such a large presence there. Our World War II ally, the Soviet Union, controlled the Eastern part of the country, and it was Winston Churchill who first put his finger on what would become the dominant threat of postwar Europe and weigh on the minds of many Americans including Newt. During his famous speech at Westminster College, Churchill warned,

> *"From Stettin in the Baltic to Trieste in the Adriatic, an iron curtain has descended across the Continent. Behind that line lie all the capitals of the ancient states of Central and Eastern Europe. Warsaw, Berlin, Prague, Vienna, Budapest, Belgrade, Bucharest, and Sofia, all these famous cities and the populations around them lie in what I must call the Soviet sphere, and all are subject, in one form or another, not only to Soviet influence but to a very high, and, in many cases, increasing measure of control from Moscow."*

In many respects the mission in Asia and the mission in Europe were the same—to prevent those continents from going Communist. The only difference was that Korea was an actual active war zone, and the European continent was in

*Newt in
Paris (1952)*

the throes of what became known as the Cold War. Of course, from the perspective of physical survival, Newt had received a favorable lot.

Newt had said good-bye to his friend Norm Diamond before embarking for Europe. Little did the two of them realize that Norm would soon be joining him there, as he too would be activated and stationed at a nearby base. Norm bought an

Newt and fellow ping pong champions. He was a very good
ping pong player his whole life and had great mastery of spins.

automobile from a GI who was returning stateside, and Norm
and Newt would spend their off time tooling around all over
Germany and in some nearby countries. There was much
to see, especially for someone who had scarcely been out
of Northeast Ohio, and the postcards that Newt would send

home attested that their travels were a portal into a world that went back well into Medieval times.

Of all Newt's adventures in Germany, none would make such a deep impression on him as the trip he made to Dachau Concentration Camp, not much more than six years after its liberation. Newt's first wife, Sally Becker Wade, still remembers the impact it had on him:

> *"I remember Newt describing to me how spotlessly clean it was. One of the buildings reminded him of the Cumberland Swimming Pool, which was a place in Cleveland that we all loved to go to. Why did it remind him of the pool? It had these white tile walls, and the fact that such a place as that, a place of human horror, could remind him of a place that he associated with fun, well, it just made a tremendous impression on him. He told me that he promised himself, "I have to do whatever I can to make sure that this never happens again."*

Newt told many others about another lesson he learned from that visit and the striking similarity of the buildings of the concentration camp and the Cumberland Swimming Pool. Newt realized that the "evil" was not in the buildings. The evil resided in men's minds. It was their belief system, their ideology, that was responsible for the horrific actions of the Nazis, not their infrastructure or technology. This was a simple but shocking realization.

This understanding did not have immediate consequences, but much later in life, it became a guiding principle for his philanthropy. He spoke about fighting the war of ideas so that the war of bullets, bombs, and concentration camps would not have to be fought. As we'll see, Newt's philanthropy focused on think tanks, and advocacy/educational organizations that spoke to many different audiences in ways that each could understand, but all with the ultimate goal of fighting the war of ideas and protecting the Jewish people and Western civilization.

There were other destinations of note. September of 1951 found him, in of all places, Nuremberg, attending High Holiday services run by the Jewish chaplains of the U.S. Army. He no doubt walked on the grounds where the Nazis held their big party meetings and rallies, which in September 1933 and 1934 were the subject for Leni Riefenstahl's famous piece of Nazi propaganda, *Triumph of the Will*. Nuremberg was also the city in which, after the party rally the following year, the Nazi racial laws, known as the Nuremberg Laws, were imposed. Of being in such an infamous city, Newt wrote to his brother Phil, "Spent the New Year in services in Nuremberg. Between services, I toured the 'Walled City' and the 'Palace of Justice,' where Goring and the rest of the Nazi war criminals were tried."

It was not only in visiting the places of the distant and recent past which clearly affected Newt, but one could posit that watching the changes that had taken place in postwar Germany must have left its mark on the young soldier. West Germany, which had just been created in 1949, would not fully achieve sovereignty until 1955. This was a creation from the events of World War II, which did not end like the first one. There was no peace treaty like the Treaty of Versailles, simply an unconditional surrender with four zones of occupation. It was not until Newt was stationed in Germany that the United States rescinded its Declaration of War, which was in force for a full decade. The Marshall Plan, designed to rebuild Europe after the war, formally ended that year.

Perhaps the greatest thing that Newt Becker saw that year was not the rebuilding of Europe economically but the restoration of German democracy. To be able to establish a viable democracy from the monstrosity of totalitarian rule was no small achievement. Indeed, it is something that Russia would also struggle with years later after the fall of the Soviet Union. To be sure, Germany had a short and sordid history democratically, and many felt that the Teutonic mindset and its strong military and authoritarian tradition were inconsistent with the building up of liberal democracy. Whether due to worries over the potential Soviet threat and a return to totalitarianism or the strong American occupation and the leadership of Konrad Adenauer, Newt saw that democracy did, in fact, take a foothold in a country without such a previous tradition. For someone so invested in democracy, both its defense against extremism and the spread of democracy to countries without a previous history of strong democratic institutions, I certainly believe that Newt not only would have noticed these changes in 1951 and 1952, but would have drawn on those memories decades later.

THANKSGIVING, 1952

Newt, back from Germany, recently released from service in late May or early June of 1952, was, like so many returning servicemen, anxious to get his life back on track. He re-enrolled at Kent State for summer school and finished the coursework necessary for his degree. But part of getting his life back on track meant finding the right woman, and he was

Newt and Sally on their wedding day, November 27, 1952

aided in this matter by having the right friend. Newt had a friend who had dated a young woman named Sally Sandson. While the relationship did not work for them, the friend thought she might hit it off with Newt and so gave him her phone number. Unabashedly, he phoned her, and it was through another friend that he was able to impress her. Newt

Sally and Newt (top) on their wedding day with, from left,
Newt's aunt Esther Schlachter, Newt's mother Rebecca Grossman,
Newt's brother Phil Brodax, Newt's Uncle Jack Becker,
Newt's sister-in-law Lois Brodax.

told the nineteen-year-old home economics major at Western Reserve University (now Case Western Reserve) that he had a friend who had a sailboat and wanted to know if she would be interested in going out sailing with them on Sunday. How could she refuse such a special excursion? She said yes, and a few months later when he asked her to marry him, she said yes again.

On November 8, 1952, outgoing president Harry S. Truman, issued his last Thanksgiving proclamation.

"In the cycle of seasons, another year marked by the abundance of God's gifts is nearing its end. At such a time we are wont to turn to Him and with humble hearts to offer thanks as a Nation for his manifold blessings. . . .

We are grateful for the privileges and rights inherent in our way of life, and in particular for the basic freedoms, which our citizens can enjoy without fear. This year it is especially fitting that we offer a prayer of gratitude for the spirit of unity which binds together all parts of our country and makes us one nation indivisible."

No one would echo that sentiment more than Newt Becker, not just in 1952, but throughout his life. Newt had plenty to be thankful for as Thanksgiving Day approached. He returned home safely from service, was transformed by what he saw in Germany, became the first in his family to obtain a college degree, got engaged, and landed a job at what he considered the most prestigious accounting firm: Price Waterhouse.

On Thanksgiving Day, November 27, 1952, the wedding of Newton Becker and Sally Sandson took place at the Sandson family home. It was a small gathering; just thirteen immediate family members were present. There was, of course, a reason for that. Sally's parents had offered the young couple the choice of a big wedding or having an entire apartment properly furnished. Ever the practical couple, they chose the latter. Newt had worked for Price Waterhouse for only a few months and Newt and Sally had very few material possessions.

PRICE WATERHOUSE

"He is Jewish but doesn't look it."

Those were the written comments of the interviewer at Price Waterhouse. How do we know? When Newt was honored by Kent State in 1984 one of the speakers was John O'Brien, a managing partner at Price Waterhouse. Given his position at the firm, John had access to the personnel files and looked through them in preparation for the Kent State event. While speaking with him as material was gathered for this book, he related this comment.

For the younger readers of this book, such a comment must seem shockingly politically incorrect and it must seem a little odd to be concerned about an accountant's Jewishness. After all, today when one hears of a Jewish accountant the two words together almost seem redundant. The big accounting firms (once known as the Big Eight, they are now down to the Big Four) today are filled with Jews. Many of the partners are Jewish, and they make every effort to accommodate their Jewish employees, particularly their traditionally oriented ones, in matters of diet and holidays.

It was not always so. Jews were once restricted or severely inhibited from entering the workforce in the hallowed halls of firms such as Price Waterhouse. And it was not just the accounting firms but the commercial banks and many of the large companies. Likewise, there were quotas that restricted Jewish enrollment in prestigious universities and professional schools. It was a rigged game, and it was only after World War II and continuing through the 1950s and 1960s that things began to loosen up a bit.

Newt Becker interviewed only with Price Waterhouse. He figured he would start with the top firm and work his way down. He never had to, as they offered him a job—the only Jewish accountant on a staff of about 70 accountants and perhaps the first Jewish accountant at its Cleveland office. At times, in remarks to his friends, Newt referred to himself as the "Show Jew"—his phrase for a token minority.

The firm had three founders, Samuel Price, William Hopkins Holyland, and Edwin Waterhouse. They started their partnership in London in 1865, so the firm had deep roots and had long expanded throughout Europe and North America. While it was not British in any real sense, it was formal and somewhat stiff. The dress code in 1952 was straight out of Brooks Brothers—suits in only the darkest hues of gray, blue, and, of course, the ever-popular black. Pinstripes were prohibited as were blue shirts. Ties were of the old-school variety, and no short sleeves, please. While the expression "rolling up your shirt sleeves" seems tailor-made for an accounting firm, it was a no-go at Price Waterhouse, or at least in the firm's office. While at a client's office, Price Waterhouse accountants were permitted to roll theirs up only if there was a separate and distinct area reserved for the accountants to work in. Forget about Casual Fridays!

Not looking Jewish meant Newt was acceptable not only to the powers that be at Price but to their clients, many of whom were large companies. Of course, despite the seemingly stodgy tone of the firm, its people were not lacking in a sense of humor. One of the standard questions in job interviews at large accounting firms is "Would you be willing to travel?" to which the standard response, at least in that era, would have been an emphatic and enthusiastic yes. Newt's clever retort was, "Yes, but not very far," and it seemed to endear him to the interviewer. After all, the young man was not only clever and congenial, but confident enough in himself to risk such an answer.

Price pushed its young associates hard, and the stereotype of the boring number cruncher could not have been further from reality. Though the guys, and we say *guys* because to my knowledge all of the associates in 1952 were men, worked hard they seemed to have earned a reputation for playing just as hard. Sally remembers entertaining them in their home and having to figure on a fifth of the liquor of choice per person. That is a rather stunning amount, and, as most Jews generally eschewed heavy social drinking, Newt and Sally did their best to accommodate. Newt took to scotch, as he did not like it much, and, therefore, thought it would provide the greatest opportunity to nurse his drink over the course of an evening. He found that cultural attitudes aside, he began to like it and had to discover other means of limiting his consumption. On those few occasions, especially when out of town for an audit and out with the guys, when he may have overindulged he felt it the next day, whereas his colleagues seemed to experience few aftereffects.

Alcohol was not the only thing that made him feel different. One night at a firm dinner the entrée, and the only entrée, served was baked ham. Just as his attitude toward alcohol reflected the traditional Eastern European home that he came from, so too his attitude toward some foods, particularly ham and pork. It was not necessarily based on ritual belief or practice but rather deeply embedded in his psyche, just as it had been collectively going back to the Hanukkah

Passover 1954, from left, Sally's brother-in-law Vic Kupps, Sally's sister Joanie Kupps, Sally's mother Bea Sandson, Sally, Newt, and seated Sally's grandmother Anna Price, and grandfather Joseph Price.

story where Hannah and her seven sons were forced by the Greek king to eat swine. As the tale has been told for over 2,000 years, they martyred themselves, and while Newt was facing a far different circumstance, he was no less resistant. He thought it terribly inconsiderate of them to serve a food that most non-Jews know Jews traditionally do not eat. He arrived home that evening furious and no doubt hungry, and perhaps the latter further fueled the former. Whether the fare that night was a deliberate dig or merely an innocuous oversight, we will never know. But it points to Newt's feeling of being a bit of an outsider—that while deeply liked within the firm, he was still the token Jew. While it may have brought out some anger and resentment, it also likely brought out many of Newt's finer ethical qualities. Many of his associates had little contact with Jews, and the fine impression that he made, both in and out of the office, no doubt impacted their approach to those of the Mosaic persuasion.

PROJECT CONVERTIBLE

Some men see things as they are and ask why. Others dream of things that never were and ask why not.
                                        —*George Bernard Shaw*

Don't undertake a project unless it is manifestly important and nearly impossible.
                                        —*Edwin Land*

Throughout interviews for this book, many people, be they family, friends, or those in organizations that Newt was involved with, pointed to Newt's love of projects. Irwin Field, a leading Los Angeles businessman and philanthropist who worked with Newt on a variety of projects described his penchant for projects the best: "When it came to a project that interested him, Newt was like a dog with a new bone. Once he got his teeth in it, he was not going to let it go."

Like so many men of the postwar generation, Newt had a genuine appreciation of convertible automobiles. I speak here of those cars whose vinyl hood comes down or off and leaves passengers exposed to the open air. Ideal for cruising around in the sweet sunshine with a balmy breeze around you, for

Newt and Sally's house on Wendy Drive (summer 1954-summer 1960)
where all three children were born.

some it can combine two loves: cars and nature. Of course, when the weather is not so nice, either unusually hot or unseasonably cold, you have the option of putting the roof up. This is all best suited for Southern California weather which is full of warm and sunny days and offers little in the way of extremes. When it comes to the city of Cleveland, Ohio, however, with hot summers and long and tough winters filled with all kinds of foul precipitation, convertibles are far from ideal. But Newt was not deterred by impediments, and, as soon as he was financially able, he purchased a convertible for himself and would eventually get one for Sally as well.

Newt would frequently drive it around in the summer, sans top, with the air conditioning going, and, when it got cold, with the heat fully turned on. But he started to think about the situation. During the winter, the fabric of the convertible is particularly vulnerable to snow, sleet, freezing rain, and high winds coming off Lake Erie. Why was there no such thing as a detachable hardtop that could be put on a convertible when the weather required it? It should be mentioned that only one of the many convertible models had the hardtop, and that was the Ford Thunderbird. Otherwise, you were out of luck.

As George Bernard Shaw noted above, "some people dream of things that never were and ask why not?" Newt was one of those guys, and, as he dreamt of convertible hardtops, he thought "Why not?" He had a collaborator on this particular project, Norm Jacobson, a chemical engineer and friend. Presumably, Norm brought the engineering skills to the table, and Newt everything else. The two men spent nearly every weekend together over an extended time trying all manner of different approaches. They got as far as coming up with some kind of a prototype, but it never went beyond that. Newt's dream of a hardtop convertible for all convertible models remained a dream, but it would be one of many, many dreams and several would be actualized in time. He would realize his first big success with the founding of what would become known as the Becker CPA Review Course.

CHAPTER THREE

The Founding of Becker CPA Review

BECOMING A CPA

CPA stands for certified public accountant. It is a designation that is conferred on passing what is commonly known as the CPA Exam. During most of Newt's career, the exam itself was a 19½-hour, four-part exam taken over 2½ days. The breakdown of the individual parts was Auditing (3½ hours), Accounting Theory (3½ hours), Business Law (3½ hours), and Accounting Practice (9 hours). To the non-accountant, the whole ordeal seems intimidating enough. To those in the field, particularly on their first try, the exam has the reputation of being about as pleasant as a stroll through "Dante's Inferno." To those who are both lawyers and accountants and have taken the bar exam and the CPA exam, most are quick to point out that compared to the CPA exam, the bar exam is a walk in the park.

There is a central difference between the CPA and bar exams, as well. One may not legally practice law in one's state unless one has passed the bar exam. One may practice accounting without taking the CPA exam; however, one may not certify financial statements for a public company or certify audits for such companies unless one is a CPA. That is only part of the story. The CPA credential carries with it a great deal of prestige, and certainly anyone working in public accounting eventually needs to become a CPA.

This brings us to Newt. In his day, it was expected of all associates at big accounting firms to sit for the exam after several years of working for the firm. It was then likely to take a number of years to pass all four parts of the exam with a required passing grade of at least 75 on each section. Most candidates do not pass all four parts on the first try, and Newt was no exception. Many stories told from Becker CPA Review Course instructors and Price Waterhouse colleagues have focused on Newt's not passing the exam, and there has been some speculation about how many tries it took him to pass all four parts. The best information available is that three times was apparently the charm, and he had longtime associates in the field who would kid him about this shortcoming over the years. His retort was classic Newt: "I didn't have the benefit of Becker CPA Review." Of course, this was only partly true because during his own preparation for the exam, he was building Becker without knowing it. He had clearly felt some pressure over the exam and really buckled down, preparing work papers for it that were to serve him well when he started Becker and applied his marvelously analytic mind to understanding the test. Newt was doing more than *studying for the exam*; he was actually *studying the exam*, noting the frequency of questions from year to year. This he was able to do because at that time the questions were released every year. Newt must have been very pleased indeed when he received the results. Not only did he pass, but the score was very high. He had proved right the old military adage, "Proper preparation prevents poor performance," and took note of the methodology and the material that was responsible.

There were two groups at Price Waterhouse who also took note of his newfound success. Of course, the partners were interested, but none was more impressed than his fellow associates, in particular those who had not yet passed the exam. It should have all ended there. Newt should have been happy to have a competitive edge over some of the other associates. The other associates were curious to know how he managed to pull it off, and Newt volunteered to share with his colleagues how they could potentially do just as well. The fact that he was willing to spend his own time without any tangible reward helping others improve their test scores cannot be emphasized enough. It points to something very deep in his character. Though he still remained focused on his own success, he was also interested in helping and teaching other people. That equation would be the cornerstone of his future success—improving his own lot as a result of helping other people improve theirs.

There were takers of his offer to help, so Newt helped his fellow associates with the material on the weekends. He employed his work papers and some of his strategies, though it seems to have been on a somewhat intermittent basis. The firm allowed them to use the library for the sessions and it was that year of 1957 which unofficially marks the beginning of Becker CPA. Well, it all worked beautifully, and the pass rate for the young associates improved enough for the higher ups to make inquiries. When told that Newt was behind the success, they allowed him to teach on company time. That is not to say that they were paying him extra to teach, but his time spent teaching would be considered billable hours.

His career at Price Waterhouse was advancing. One of the clients whom he had brought into the firm was the bottling company, Miller Becker. As mentioned in the first chapter, Miller Becker was a virtual institution in Ohio, and was started by his Uncle Eli and Eli's partner who also hailed from Lapy, Poland. The company had grown over the years to employ several hundred people and their pride and joy was their gin- ger ale named The Cotton Club, which evoked all manner of fizzy fun. Its success was the pride and joy of the family and it must have been enormously satisfying for Newt to have the company as a client. Though his Uncle Eli had already passed away, his cousin Martin was running the firm, and it was a sign that the poor relation had arrived. Martin's son, Eli, named for his grandfather, who would eventually serve the firm as the company's treasurer, told me that they kept some of Newt's work papers around, and using Newt was not just a matter of helping a relative. They had great respect for Newt as an accountant and it seems that this opinion was shared by all who came into contact with him in those years at Price Waterhouse. Newt had risen from associate to senior accoun- tant and was heading up some jobs. He had also earned an MBA in 1958 at Western Reserve University. His professional career was not the only area of his life that was expanding. The Becker family balance sheet had added three major assets with David being born in 1954, Laura in 1956, and Daniel, four years later.

It was not all work and family. Though the two occupied much of his time, there was another passion. Newt did not come to philanthropy in his middle years like so many do; he was right there in his twenties when he assumed his first mantle of leadership: chairman of the Young Adults Division of the Jewish Federation of Greater Cleveland. At this relatively young age, he was now in the company of some of the most powerful of his co-religionists as he attended meetings and other events. You remember when he asked, "What are the rich Jews doing to protect us?" Well, now he was in their company on a regular basis, and it had one fundamental impact. At the annual campaign event, these men would announce their pledge for the following year. Whether Newt felt inspired or emboldened or both, he would increase his pledge significantly over the previous year. Apparently, he was not one to say, "Same as last year, plus *chai*." The word for life in Hebrew is *chai*, which has a numerical value of eighteen. It is common for people to use chai as a denomination when giving to Jewish or other causes. Not Newt, for he would always push himself to make ever more significant commitments though Sally would fret over their ability to meet them, since they had barely met the pledge from the previous year.

THE DECISION TO LEAVE PRICE WATERHOUSE

As the decade of the 1960s loomed, Newt Becker found himself at a crossroads. Though he was a senior accountant, he was still a good number of years removed from making partner. There must have been some question in his mind of whether a firm that had only recently begun to hire Jews was ready for a Jewish partner. Even if that were to happen, there was the question of whether he would want to spend his career in public accounting, and, if so, did he want to work for a Big Eight firm?

One of the career options for people in Newt's situation was to leave public accounting and go to work for an operating company. That often develops naturally enough as clients get so comfortable with their accountant that they ask him to join their company in a financial capacity. At this point in Newt's career, he had the requisite experience to interview for a controller's position, the chief accounting officer in a corporation. If successful in that position, presumably he could be promoted up the ladder to the top post in finance, the chief financial officer. From CFO he could even end up as CEO. Newt was obviously qualified to interview for a corporate controller job. Besides his noteworthy skills as an accountant, he was an MBA. Needless to say, he was also a CPA.

Cleveland in the late 1950s had plenty of growing companies but one of the most creative and innovative companies in the area was named American Greeting Cards. It was the number two player in the field, trailing only behind the behemoth Hallmark Corporation.

American Greeting Cards had the kind of story behind it that mirrored Newt's own. Though its name and its niche sound thoroughly American, it was, in fact, the creation of an immigrant from Eastern Europe. Jacob Sapirstein arrived in America in 1905 and eventually made his way to Cleveland where he earned his keep selling post cards. With a $50 loan as startup capital, he began his own line of post cards and greeting cards, and by the time he left this world at the age of 102, the $50 loan had turned into a company that was doing over $1 billion in sales. Not too shabby, and, in fact, when Newt interviewed for the controller's job, the company had already gone public, making his CPA credential even more valuable. Despite its large size, American Greeting Cards was still at its core a family business. Irving Stone, Jacob Sapirstein's son, had changed the family name and the rest of the family followed suit. He ran the company, with his father serving as chairman. Though they had anglicized their name, the family was hardly composed of assimilated Jews. Like Newt Becker they were highly committed Jews and they were highly philanthropic, both locally and for Israel. A neighborhood outside of Jerusalem, Telz-Stone, is named for Irving Stone; the family sponsored a well-known version of the Pentateuch, simply called the *Stone Chumash*, which is in popular use in hundreds of American synagogues. So while Newt was in fact offered the job, one thing he would not have to worry about is being served baked ham at a company dinner.

While his Jewishness would not have been an impediment to advancement at American Greeting Cards, there were other factors to consider. Although a look at the company's webpage fifty-plus years later reveals that there are plenty of outsiders in senior positions, the top slots in the company are still run by family members, including those who married into the family. When Newt was offered the job, one of those family members was studying accounting in college. The concern was that there was a significant chance that Newt would spend a number of years on the job only to train his replacement. On the one hand, that would not be so bad if he were to be moved up. On the other hand, there was always the possibility that he might be out of a job.

One of the major considerations in looking at taking a new job was salary. And the increase in pay that was being offered over what Newt was earning at Price Waterhouse was considerable. On the other hand, the question that Newt had to ask himself was, would he ever be happy there as an employee, albeit it a highly paid one? One suspects that in the end that was the critical factor in his declining to join American Greeting Cards and turning down similar opportunities. In the end, Newt made the decision to leave Price Waterhouse after seven years, not to join an operating company or a smaller accounting firm, but rather to choose a path that would define his professional and business career; from then on he would be his own boss. In 1959, at the age of 30, that meant that he would be hanging out his shingle as Newton D. Becker & Co., Certified Public Accountants.

Going out on his own was a risk, but it was somewhat mitigated by one very significant factor; he had already recruited a client. A businessman who was a friend of his father-in-law was in urgent need of an accountant and was sufficiently impressed by Newt to give him a shot. From there, Newt would need to come up with some other clients in order to build a practice. One client was not nearly enough to support the family and as time passed Newt looked for a way to supplement his income.

THE BEGINNING OF BECKER CPA REVIEW

It was only a few months since he had left the employ of Price Waterhouse, and because of that his teaching had come to an

PR 1-2451   STANDARD BUILDING
                                  CLEVELAND

Newton D. Becker & Co.
Certified Public Accountants

NEWTON D. BECKER, BS, MBA, CPA

end. He had not planned on teaching independently, but just then, as economic pressure loomed, he wondered what if he got a group of guys from the firm to make use of his services? Sure, he would not be able to use the library at the firm anymore, but he could rent a room at night or on the weekends, and if he could just convince the guys to pay him for something that previously had been free, he could survive until his accounting practice took off.

There was something else at work here. Before he left Price Waterhouse, one of the firm's more senior accountants had suggested that Newt's teaching might actually be a real business. As the necessity of earning an income came fully into play, the words of that individual began to sound better and better. Perhaps there was really something there.

A minyan (a prayer quorum in Judaism) requires ten men, and, in 1960, Newt was able to round up ten fellows who said yes. At $100 a head, Newt had some money coming in, and he basically just continued what he had been doing before. He found an inexpensive downtown location and he really did not incur a lot of expenses as he started teaching.

A NATURAL TEACHER

"Those who can, do; those who can't, teach." Those of us who are current and former teachers, this writer included, take great exception to that statement. While it may have some truth in some areas, one of the reasons that Newt was such a good teacher of the CPA material was that he was an excellent accountant. He understood how an accountant looked at the material, but he combined it with an out-of-the-box mentality that allowed him to look at the test itself, in a unique and refreshing way. It must be said that in a sense this was one of the things that made him an original. While he had an accountant's eye for detail, he had the mindset of a totally different kind. Though he relied on his written material and lectures, he understood half a century ago the importance of the interaction between teacher and student which he never forgot even in something as structured and formalized as his course.

For now, he was teaching the four different parts of the CPA exam and word began to spread. His best promoters were his students themselves. Soon Newt began to analyze not only the CPA exam but his pass rate and how to maximize it. Newt understood that the key to promoting his course was to provide hard data of pass rates. He did not play on the fear or the anxiety of his students, but rather sought to assuage it and give them the confidence they needed to pass.

With Cleveland as his base, he began teaching classes to a group in Columbus. The commute was long, close to 150 miles, so he taught only the largest section, Accounting Practice. He realized that the main impediment to further expansion was the limitation that there was only one Newt Becker, and that one Newt Becker could be in only one place at one time—but maybe that was not quite so.

Newt would enjoy a lifelong love affair with technology and how it can make one's life more productive and efficient when properly used. The future of his business was in some manner a direct result of the hard creative work of a lot of people who, starting in the nineteenth century, began the process of recording sound. Thomas Edison was one, but Newt owes a debt of gratitude to the little-known Merle Duston, who in the 1930s applied for US Patent Number 556,743, Method of and Apparatus for Recording Sound and Other Vibrations. The tape recorder turned out to be a very important invention and was very practical and enjoyed by many, perhaps none more so than Newt Becker.

Thirty years after Duston, Newt used the recording technology to help students who had missed a class. They could come in on another night (Newt would be teaching all four sections during the week) and listen to the class they had missed using one of the reel-to-reel tapes. Newt had recorded all his classes just for this purpose, and one night there was a particularly attentive student sitting in the back of the class listening to his lecture, glued to a pair of earphones. The class broke every night for much-needed coffee and donuts. One night Newt noticed that the man listening to the recorder did not shut the thing off and adjourn with the rest the group. Thinking that the young man needed the break as much as anyone, he went over to him and suggested to him that he join in on the caffeine and the sweets. The man said he could not take a break. Why? Newt asked. Because it's not time for the break on tape, was the response of this young man, who was seemingly oblivious to what was going on outside of the world of the recorder and the voice of Newt Becker.

That was the first "Aha!" moment. An epiphany of sorts, Newt realized that the recorder might be something that could be used for more than just helping students catch up on a class they had missed. A second moment of Eureka came when students from Columbus, who were anxious for instruction in the other three parts of the exam, came to him with a request: "Listen, we know that it's hard for you to drive down here when you are teaching in Cleveland, but why don't you make the tapes up for us of the other three parts? We will rent a room and listen to it among ourselves." They were willing to pay, and it sounded like a great idea, so he gave them both the tapes and written materials on all three subjects.

The question was how would they do without him to guide them? Could it be done without his physical presence? He would not know the answer until the results came in from the powers in Columbus, who graded the CPA exam. Well, they came in, and guess what? His students in Columbus performed just as well as the students did in Cleveland. Newt knew how to look at data, and he wanted to make sure that this was not a statistical anomaly. He looked at it six ways to Sunday, and there was no mistaking the results. He was looking at the potential for a scalable business here, and if he could hire someone to run the class using his recordings, projected visuals, and handouts, and who could answer questions, he was in business. The recorder would essentially allow Newt to clone himself, and his voice would eventually be heard from Miami to Seattle, and then around the world, as if he were in every place at the same time. His unique voice was ubiquitous in the world of accounting, and many recognized it instantly when they met him for the first time.

Thus, what was initially meant to be only a supplement to his accounting practice was soon to be his main thing. His accounting practice took a backseat to what would become known as the Becker CPA Review Course—or just "Becker."

THE BECKER TEACHING METHOD

Newt was, at heart, an educator. As such, he had his own unique pedagogical approach and methodology. In many ways, he was inspired by ideas from Behaviorism in psychology and by "programmed learning" that was being explored with computer interfaces, but he developed his own creative application of these principles.

The Becker teaching method evolved and systematized over time, but from the time he began to use recordings, it involved four main elements: a recording of Newt's voice; projected visuals on a very large screen; class handouts that were an integral part of the instruction during the class; and the in-person instructor who brought the whole thing alive.

Projected Visuals: Even when Newt was teaching all of his classes himself, he used projected visuals to present new information concisely and to provide many examples that could be worked through as part of the class session. The overhead projector with clear 10"×12" transparencies was clearly the best method available during the years Newt ran Becker, which was well before the era of computer generated graphics. He purchased the best overhead projectors available which made it possible to project very bright and very large images that could be easily seen in the back of a room full of 150 students *and with the lights on* (which was important for allowing students to take notes and for keeping them awake!). In addition, the images were so large that many lines of text could be used on each transparency, unlike a regular slide projector that could include only a few lines of text. For most of his career, Newt hand lettered his own transparencies (which he usually called "slides" for short) with a very bold pen designed for writing on transparencies. The thick lines of the bold pen provided clarity for those seated at the back of the room. The hand-lettered transparencies were used as "masters" for duplication.

Once Newt began using the recordings, he realized that there should always be something for the students to look at, thus he added additional slides so that there was always something on the screen that related to the lecture. His intuition anticipated the later recognition that some people learn better visually and others learn better by auditory presentation. The content of the slides ranged from point by point presentations of accounting rules (always followed by an explanation and example), to flow charts, to examples of working through complex problems, to sample multiple choice questions taken from recent exams. He also included cartoons, most of which came from the newspaper and provided occasional notes of humor loosely tied to the content of the lecture.

Newt also realized that it was important to reveal only the portion of the slide that dealt with the specific point he was making. He did not want students reading the whole slide and then tuning out during the explanation. His practice was to cover most of the slide and then to slowly reveal it, line by line, as each new point was discussed.

Newt (about 1966)

Class handouts: Newt wanted to make sure that students had good notes to study from, and didn't want to count on the ability of every student to take notes on the most important material. He prepared handouts that included an outline of the key points of each lecture, and the class presentations were spent walking through those outlines. By the end of each class, the student had gone through every line of the outline, and had heard additional explanations and examples, and now knew precisely what each line meant. When he or she studied from the outline later, it was a form of *reviewing* material, not seeing it for the first time.

Recording of Newt's lecture: When Newt was teaching all of his classes live in the early years, he noticed that because he had so much information on the screen and handouts, and because Newt was *seated* next to the projector to change transparencies, students didn't look at him very often when he was speaking: they were usually looking at the screen or their handouts as they jotted down notes. Once he started recording his lectures, he found that the students' experience was not that different while listening to the recording compared to listening to him lecture live. As long as there was something with content to look at, his moving lips were irrelevant. He was a very firm believer in the importance of recording the lectures in front of a regular classroom with live students. He knew that instructors speaking to an empty studio gave a different kind of presentation than those who taught with live students present. The recordings in front of a live audience were warmer, more interactive and had more realistic pacing. The audio quality probably suffered slightly, but that was not really an issue. The students who listened to the recordings heard the same lecture that the students heard when Newt presented the material live, and the sound came through the same speakers using the same PA system that Newt used to amplify his voice when teaching live.

The live instructor: By putting so much of the content of the course on the recording, the slides, and the handouts, this made it possible to hire instructors who were not account-ing professors and who could bring real-world experience and an effective teaching personality to the classroom. Of course, the instructors needed to be able to operate the tape recorder and overhead projector, but their bigger role was in managing the class, clarifying any of Newt's lecture that needed explanation, adding additional content, and answer-ing students' questions.

They were assisted in the classroom by a document called the "J-Notes," or Interject Notes, for each session. The J-Notes were 8½"×14" sheets that had two columns. The right col-umn showed a transcript of the recording and indicated exactly when each transparency should appear. The left col-umn was for notes for the instructor, ranging from specific procedural advice (e.g., stop the tape for 7 minutes to allow students to work a specific exercise) to advice about content (e.g., explain why choice "b" is better than choice "d" on this multiple choice question). The left column also had plenty of space for the instructor to jot down his own notes for points that he or she wanted to bring up in the session, and made it easy for the instructor to know exactly when to pause the tape and to interject his or her point. Instructor interjects often included elaboration on Newt's points and real world exam-ples of issues.

Most of the content of the course was presented by Newt using the audio visual materials, and this methodology ensured that the students would get a good experience and would learn the material even if the instructor was not the greatest. On the other hand, the rating system of the instructors helped ensure that the vast majority of them were skilled teachers. The live instructors always referred to "Newt" and never to "the tape" and they were able to create the feeling of a course that was *team taught* by two instructors. They could take the course from a good experience to an excellent one.

Newt also understood that another key to keeping the student engaged was to make sure that the student always had something active to do in addition to listening to Newt's voice and watching his slides on the big screen. The lectures were constantly broken up by multiple choice questions that required the students to raise their hand and vote on a choice, and by instructions to write down a note; to circle or underline a word or phrase; or put stars next to important points on the handouts; or to look at something specific on the screen. If a student started to drift off, within a minute or two he would be pulled back to the lecture by having to do something active. Each lecture also featured longer periods where the recording was stopped while students worked on longer exercises and problems. When the recording resumed, those exercises and problems would be reviewed by Newt and specific issues and concerns would be fielded by the live instructor.

Newt always believed that his instructional method combined the advantages of live instruction with the benefits of a thoroughly prepared and tested presentation that provided excellent quality control for his classrooms. Of course, his competition tried to denigrate this method as impersonal and mechanical. One of his competitors prepared a poster called "Real or Reel?" with two photos side by side. On the left was a photo of one of their live instructors and on the right was a photo of a giant reel-to-reel tape recorder standing on a table at the front of the room with a blank blackboard behind it. Newt's consistent response to this issue was to offer the first few sessions of his course for free so that students could assess the course for themselves without having to commit the tuition. He knew that the course presented by his teaching method would sell itself.

It is interesting to note that from coast to coast, students felt personally connected to Newt. They knew his voice, they knew his philosophy, and they knew how vested he was in their success. What was amazing was that this personal connection was felt even by students who never met Newt. Occasionally the voice and the body would come together. Newt traveled the country making sure that the classes were meeting his standards and he maintained strong relationships with Becker instructors. He would frequently show up unannounced to the students in the middle of a class and make his surprise appearance after a break. While the tape had been his voice all along, after the break it would be the real life Newt speaking. Dramatic! The students loved it—the man and the voice now all in one!

BECKER MYTHS

One of the myths that has developed around Becker CPA is that Newt left Price Waterhouse to start Becker CPA because he recognized a unique opportunity. Though that narrative sounds plausible years later, it is not quite true. In fact, as we have seen, it is not true at all. Like so many great entrepreneurial concerns, it developed through a unique series of events that could not have been preconceived or put together in the soundest of business plans prepared by the smartest of MBAs.

Another myth seems to revolve around the meteoric expansion of Becker to what would eventually include 143 locations when Newt sold the business to DeVry in 1996. In fact, the first couple of years were actually fairly trying times for Becker CPA.

One of the reasons many potential entrepreneurs hold back from going out on their own is the very realistic fear that they will not be able to meet their financial obligations. When there's a family to think about, such fears become very real. The security of working for established firms like Price Waterhouse or American Greeting Cards could temper the spirits of all but the most determined.

Before Newt was able to expand the operation beyond his own teaching, money in the Becker household was tight. Sally's family, who were fairly comfortable, offered some assistance until Newt was doing well in what was then thought would be his accounting practice. They had grown to share Sally's optimism about Newt's future success, but having been in business for a long time themselves, understood that these things take time and did not want to see the family suffer in the short term. Newt, full of pride and confident as could be, refused to accept any financial help from his in-laws. Nonetheless, Sally's mother helped out anyway by taking her shopping, paying for groceries, and supplying her with various items that they bought in bulk Costco-style before such chains were in vogue. Again, the notion of Newt becoming an overnight success and immediately wealthy is simply a myth.

Perhaps this was another great lesson to learn from Newt. It would take the better part of a decade for his Becker CPA to establish itself.

In the early years, there was no corporate staff; in fact, there were no employees at all. Newt was a one-man show. While his neighbors headed for their downtown offices and would come home at night to be with their families, Newt would teach at night, come home and have a late dinner sometimes at 10:30 or 11:00, then get up at 9 or 10 in the morning and begin his teaching preparations and seeing to whatever tasks as were necessary to support the fledgling operation. His workspace was the family dining room table. That was when his young kids were not around doing what young kids will do. When things got a bit too noisy, Newt would head to the public library and set up shop.

For Newt, one of the appeals of Becker CPA Review, and something that kept him going through difficult times, was that he was his own boss, something which greatly suited his personality. Though it may have been a struggle in the early years, in the back of his mind was the sage advice rendered by his mother: "The only way to make real money is to have your own business."

Throughout his life, Newt felt himself fortunate in a number of ways. He was able to take something he loved and turn it into a successful career. It was a point of emphasis that he would later impart to his own children that it was very important to choose a career that they truly enjoyed. In addition to the monetary benefits that would eventually come from the Becker CPA Review Course, two elements remained constant throughout the years: he gained enormous satisfaction from crafting excellent educational materials and from the success

Becker home on Fairmont Blvd. in Shaker Heights (about 1961)

of his students. Unlike other entrepreneurs who saw themselves as destined for success, Newt believed that luck was
a necessary part of success—along with creativity, strategic
thinking, meticulousness, and plenty of hard work. He was
acquainted with many talented, hardworking individuals who
did not enjoy similar success.

After about a year of teaching his Becker CPA Review
course, Newt's income had slightly exceeded his income at
Price Waterhouse. In the summer of 1960, the Beckers moved
into a more spacious home in Shaker Heights, a very desirable
suburb which they could barely afford. Newt worked from a
desk in the master bedroom and could close the door when
he needed it quiet. While this was not a fancy home office,
Newt was a man who was not unaware or unappreciative of

what it took and what it meant to make the relatively short trip, but fairly long journey, from Glenville to Shaker Heights.

Newt and Sally divorced in November 1964 by mutual agreement. In the following decades, they continued to inter-act around their three children and six grandchildren. They were exemplary ex-spouses and maintained a friendly and caring relationship.

CALIFORNIA DREAMING

As one went to Europe to see the living past, so one must visit Southern California to observe the future.
—Alison Lurie

The call to head westward, and particularly to California, has been at the forefront of the American imagination since the Gold Rush days. In the prewar and post-war era, there was a noticeable shift that greatly increased the state's population to an almost country-like size. Besides immigrants from foreign countries, most came from the East Coast and the industrial Midwest, particularly attracted to its warm climes and sunny beaches. Jews were as likely as anyone else to want to give up the cold winters and give the Golden State a try. To give a sense of the population change regarding the Jewish commu-nity, when Newt was born in 1928, Cleveland, had more Jews than Los Angeles. By the time of his death in 2012, Los Ange-les had close to eight times as many Jews as his native city.

Going to Southern California was an attractive option for Newt and he moved to Los Angeles shortly after his divorce at age 36. Lover of convertibles that he was, it is hard to imagine that the sun, the warmth, and the ocean did not play heavily into his decision to relocate. Not surprisingly, his first apartment in 1965 was at the corner of Sunset Boulevard and Pacific Coast Highway on the edge of Malibu with a view of the ocean. He seems to have loved looking out at the vastness of the Pacific.

Newt was largely starting over. His classes continued in Ohio under the instructors whom he had trained, but his plan was to build his business in Southern California and run the operation from there. Even if he had never built the business beyond California, the state was big enough to keep him busy. Before he was able to get started there, and he borrowed money from his mother until he got established, he needed some steady income, and he took a part-time faculty position teaching accounting at the University of California Los Angeles.

This made sense for a number of reasons. In addition to the income, it would be a good base from which to set up his teaching of Becker. It would put him in touch with a large number of accounting students from which to recruit and a pool of fellow faculty members to draw on as future Becker instructors.

Newt had fully reestablished himself in Southern California and began to bring other members of his family westward. His three children would visit from Cleveland and spend the summers with him in 1965, 1966, and 1967, when they ended up staying permanently. Sally herself moved to the area that same year and Newt's mother would spend all of her later years in an apartment there, passing away in Sherman Oaks at age 96. His beloved Uncle Jack also came out and lived with Newt until he passed away. The cycle was complete when he brought out his brother Phil to work for Becker CPA Review after Phil and his wife had sold their stores in Detroit. If we go back to the late 1960s, we can say that despite the tumult that was engulfing much of the country, things were looking up for Newt Becker. He had moved to a nice home in a housing development in Malibu and would soon build his dream house in Bel Air. But one thing was still missing, a woman with whom he could share his life.

Though he had made a very smooth transition to Los Angeles, Newt was a frequent visitor to his hometown of Cleveland. He would see family and friends and, of course, check on the goings-on at the Becker classrooms. During one such visit in May 1971, several years after he had already moved to LA, Newt received a phone call from his friend, Norm Diamond. Norm wanted to know if Newt would like to join him at a party given by close friends of his. There was a reason for all of this. Norm knew that a beautiful woman named Rochelle Gordon who was newly single would be there. Newt said yes, and, when he met Rochelle the two of them hit it off immediately. Newt would later say it was love at first sight.

Of course these things are never simple when each person has children; they knew that it was important that they put their kids first. Rochelle's kids were a bit younger than Newt's. When they met, Bryan was almost 10, and Bradley almost 5—compared to David, 16, Laura, 14, and Dan, 11. Newt won them over when on his first visit when he brought them both toys including a new hot wheels car for Bryan, a highly prized item at the time. It is not difficult to understand how he became popular with the boys and they would become his children every bit as much as the ones who were his biologically. Newt asked Rochelle to marry him, she said yes, and within six months of meeting they had a small and modest ceremony in the Rabbi's study. Rochelle prepared the kids to move to Los Angeles where her sons would share a home

Rochelle and Newt
at Bryan's Bar
Mitzvah (1974)

with their three step-siblings who had a year earlier moved to Newt's newly built Bel Air home.

It would seem that at age 43, Newt finally had attained the life that he had envisioned for himself. He would spend the next four decades building his company, his philanthropy, and his character.

CHAPTER FOUR

The Business Expands

As they say, "Rome wasn't built in a day," and neither was Becker CPA. By relocating to Los Angeles, Newt was starting all over again; but he had left the Cleveland operation in good hands. Frank Prijatel, who had been an early Becker student, took over his teaching responsibilities and would eventually spearhead what would be one of the most critical elements of the teaching content: updating the materials to reflect the annual changes made to the CPA exam. As with many of the instructors, Frank would enjoy a long tenure with Becker: thirty-five years.

As we mentioned earlier, when Newt had originally begun teaching at Price Waterhouse, he never anticipated that the powers that be at the firm would allow him to bill hours for his efforts. It was then by dint of his own circumstance that he discovered people would actually pay him to teach the class. Then, through the use of the reel to reel recorder, he discovered that he could actually teach the class without being there.

Now the question was how to scale the operation and configure Becker CPA.

The instructors were key. They were more than just monitors. They needed to be able to do much more than simply run the recorder and overhead transparencies and handle administrative tasks associated with the class; they needed to have mastery over the materials and be able to answer questions. A good portion of what they were doing, in addition to teaching the material, was instilling the confidence in the students that they could pass the exam.

While most of the legions of students who took the course (going into the hundreds of thousands), would never meet Newt Becker in person, by listening to his voice they did develop a relationship with him. It was important that the instructors not only represent Becker CPA but also the ideals that Newt wanted to impart to the students. The early instructors were largely students of Newt or the students of students of his.

The instructors were part-time and held separate full-time positions outside of Becker. Most were not involved in teaching accounting full-time; they were practicing CPAs, and a good many worked for big firms. They usually became Becker instructors for reasons other than money—for the amount of money they could earn for several hours of teaching at night or on a weekend day was limited. What motivated them? They clearly believed in Newt and were committed to helping students. They remembered their own struggles with the exam and the sense of triumph they felt when they passed. It brought them the same kind of thrill that Newt got when he heard from students after they had passed and become CPAs. It is hard to place a value on the kind of satisfaction one feels from helping others not only to pass a test, but to pass a test that leads them to a more fulfilling career and a better life—not just for themselves, but for their families as well.

Being an instructor had other advantages. First, all CPAs have very strict guidelines for continuing education, requiring 120 hours every three years and a minimum of 40 hours a year to renew one's license. For Becker instructors, they could fulfill their CPE requirements through their teaching, which of course, kept them up to date on changes in the profession. There was also a benefit of status, particularly in large firms, that came with being a Becker instructor. Last, they were also part of an important network, comprising current and former Becker instructors, as well as students they got to know, some of whom would become leading figures in both accounting firms and as corporate financial executives.

There were benefits to the instructors, but, again, the allegiance that they felt to Newt was exceptional. While Newt was somewhat famous for micromanaging many things, he did allow the instructors some leeway. He monitored his students' progress, and if scores went up and down over time he looked into it. Once, he noticed that the pass rate in Seattle had gone up over time. After investigating the matter, he found that the local instructor was using three-by-five flashcards. He adopted the idea for all locations. And he paid bonuses for anyone who came up with a good idea. It might not have been much, but instructors loved the idea that they were able to make an impact. They appreciated that Newt, as much as he needed uniformity in how the class was taught, was always open to new and innovative ideas if they improved the instruction and the results.

TEST PREPARATION FIELD

Newt was a leader and innovator of what we now call the test preparation field. As we start to understand the role that Becker CPA Review played it would be helpful to understand something about the broader field of test preparation. It was a field that virtually did not exist when Newt started teaching in the late 1950s, and it was one he helped create. The field consisted of two different components: one that prepared students for entrance exams such as the SAT and LSAT; and one, like Becker CPA, that prepared students for licensing exams such as the CPA and the bar exam. The major player in entrance exams was a giant of a man whom Newt met a number of times: Stanley Kaplan. Kaplan's name was probably best known in the field, and it would never have happened if not for a quota on Jewish medical students that forced him to change career paths and become a teacher. In addition to his teaching, he had a side business tutoring students, first for the notoriously difficult New York State Regents Exam and then for the SATs. His was strictly a local New York City operation; he only thought about going national when he discovered that students were traveling from other cities to take his course. It was not until 1970, several decades after Kaplan began, that he ventured outside of New York. After building a huge national operation and expanding to include many other exams besides the SAT, he sold his company to the Washington Post Corporation in 1984 for a rather impressive forty-five million dollars.

How do you build an organization from teaching students yourself and still maintain quality and, of course, control? Newt's style was to supervise all aspects of the business and make sure that all of the operations met his standards. His

AKRON	CHICAGO	FAIRFIELD	LONG ISLAND	NEW YORK CITY	ROCHESTER	SANTA ANA
ATLANTA	CINCINNATI	FT. WORTH	LOS ANGELES	NEWARK	SACRAMENTO	SEATTLE
AUSTIN	CLEVELAND	GRAND RAPIDS	LOUISVILLE	NORFOLK	ST. LOUIS	TAMPA
BALTIMORE	COLUMBUS	HARTFORD	MEMPHIS	OKLAHOMA CITY	SALT LAKE CITY	TOLEDO
BLUE ISLAND	DALLAS	HONOLULU	MIAMI	OMAHA	SAN ANTONIO	TREVOSE
BOSTON	DAYTON	HOUSTON	MILWAUKEE	PHILADELPHIA	SAN DIEGO	TUCSON
BUFFALO	DENVER	INDIANAPOLIS	MINNEAPOLIS	PHOENIX	SAN FRANCISCO	VALLEY FORGE
CANTON	DES PLAINES	JACKSONVILLE	NASHVILLE	PITTSBURGH	SAN JOSE	VAN NUYS
CHARLESTON	DETROIT	KANSAS CITY	NEW ORLEANS	PORTLAND	SAN JUAN	WASHINGTON, D.C.
CHARLOTTE						WICHITA

HELPING ACCOUNTANTS BECOME PROFESSIONALS

BECKER CPA REVIEW

NATIONAL ADMINISTRATIVE OFFICES

15760 VENTURA BOULEVARD, 11th FLOOR
ENCINO, CALIFORNIA 91436

Becker CPA Review materials from about 1976

strength was the major metro areas, but as he entered new territories in the 1970s and 1980s, he was well aware of the pitfalls that came with expansion. He was, therefore, careful not to expand too rapidly or make the mistake of one of his competitors and franchise the operation.

Opening up a new city often was done in response to built-up demand. Newt regularly visited his classrooms, doing it in his usual unassuming manner, and this proved very inspirational for many students who got the opportunity to meet the man behind the voice. A case in point was in the early 1970s when Newt was visiting a Becker classroom in his native Cleveland and noticed there were a group of students in the class from Erie, Pennsylvania, roughly one hundred miles to the east. He suggested that they rent a bus to make their trip easier and cheaper. They responded by urging Newt to open a classroom in Erie. They won.

In thirty years since the original 1960 classroom in Cleveland, Newt would have roughly 130 classrooms in operation. He would always begin with one classroom in a city before expanding to multiple locations. He did have competitors, both regionally and nationally, but he always felt the competition made him better. In most cases, he respected his competition as in New York City where the dominant player in the market was a highly regarded professor of accounting, Sam Person, who founded Person-Wolinsky Associates Inc. in 1967. Though Newt had classrooms in New York City, he was not motivated to dislodge Person's operation. He respected him and when I spoke with Professor Person, it was clear that the respect was mutual. While competition is good because it keeps businesses on their toes, and while Newt surely believed in free market capitalism, he did not see it all as a kill or be killed type of Darwinian struggle for market share.

There was a local competitor in Southern California who was anxious to cut into Becker's piece of the pie. He would do everything possible to disrupt Newt's campus recruiting including tearing down his posters and bad-mouthing Becker CPA. Various Becker staffers became aware of the situation and urged Newt to take legal action to forestall these activities. Newt would have none of it, always taking the high road, believing his class was superior and whatever setbacks may occur in the short term as a result of this unscrupulous competitor would eventually correct themselves in the long term.

Newt's prediction came true and then some. The fellow filed for bankruptcy and left a fair amount of his organization's students without a class. What did Newt do? He allowed those left high and dry by that company to take a Becker class for free. One thing Newt refused to do was engage in a price war. Becker's sole national competitor was known for lowering prices in order to gain market share. There was pressure on Becker to respond in kind, since its prices, already the highest, were now significantly higher than the competitor's. At a meeting, a national lead instructor urged Newt to lower the prices significantly for Becker CPA Review. He would not give an inch, feeling that the important thing was to emphasize the value of the course and that overly discounting the brand would result in a dilution of it.

We should make the point that Newt instructed his people to give away the course for free or at reduced rates to those in genuine financial need, but in a noteworthy manner. Because he knew what it was like to struggle, Newt was sensitive to others' feelings and never wanted to embarass anyone. What he frequently did, so as not to make students feel guilty for accepting what amounted to a scholarship, was make them student assistants—having them help the instructor with various tasks. One of those who took advantage of Newt's graciousness ended up becoming a senior partner in one of the large national firms. He never forgot Newt's generosity.

Newt did not believe in spending a lot on the classroom facilities. He rented inexpensive spaces and poured his resources into the course content. One of his competitors rented class-room space at a plush hotel. An instructor suggested that Newt follow suit, but, as usual, he stuck to his guns and refused to change.

Another of his competitors was big on partnering with universities in offering the CPA Review Course. In such a sce-nario, the review classes would be held in conjunction with the university, presumably using their classrooms. Monies would be shared with the university, and they would in turn help promote the course among their accounting majors. While Newt realized the importance of having a good relation-ship with the universities, and specifically with the accounting professors who theoretically could also be Becker instructors, he felt that such a close relationship really amounted to a joint venture; this did not make good business sense and was not appropriate for Becker. Many universities were actually direct competitors offering their own classes. They could afford to charge less since their costs were lower, and, for an additional fee, the students could gain university credit. This will become clear when we discuss the 150-Hour Law in Chapter 5 and was an added benefit to the student. One school, the Univer-sity of Northern Illinois, has an excellent reputation in the area—having been at it for over forty years—and offers the program beyond its own campus. It didn't bother Newt that it was operating on his turf. As we discussed, he had a positive outlook on competition and felt it kept him and Becker CPA on their toes.

One of the obstacles to maintaining a dominant market presence was that the barrier to entry was fairly low. After all, one only had to look at how Newt himself started, and plenty of others had the same idea he did—only *after* he did. One

Newt and his son Dan at Dan's Confirmation party (1977)

Newt and Rochelle (1977)

Newt and his mother Rebecca (1977)

Newt and Rochelle at David's graduation from UC Berkeley (1977)

competitor had been a former Becker student who apparently really liked the Becker material. So much so that, by modifying it a bit, he created a course that was eerily similar to the one he had just taken. Again, some suggested Newt use legal means to defend his intellectual property. Much to their chagrin, but not surprise, Newt refused to take legal action.

Newt Becker simply had great confidence in his product. Although he did not disparage others, his self-confidence meant he felt he could withstand whatever competitive pressures might arise in the marketplace. Part of his confidence came from the business model that he had implemented. It was not a standard model, but it reflected the unique individual nature of its creator.

LEAN AND AGILE

Building Becker CPA meant building an organization comprising two separate components, one based in the field, and one based in the company's headquarters in Encino, California. Newt had a very strong operating philosophy, and, despite the growth that the company experienced, that operating philosophy seemed to change very little. First of all, it was a company in which every significant decision was made by Newt himself. Though you will meet a few of the key personnel who played prominent roles in the company, during Newt's time there were no other senior executives nor was there ever a strong number-two person at Becker.

Newt also had one other feature that was very rare among executives or business owners. Though he employed the usual support people including secretarial and clerical staff, he did not have an executive assistant the way most people would in his position. This is especially compelling since he was involved not only in Becker, but in many other businesses and philanthropic activities as well. For a person who was busy with so many commitments he was quite unusual in that he kept his own schedule. Even those who remain in control of virtually everything allow for an executive assistant in the name of efficiency and perhaps to serve as a buffer. Newt always remained accessible, answering his own phone, whether in the office or while working out of his home.

The corporate staff was extra lean. Accounting handled payables and receivables as well as payroll and human resources. There was Educational Materials, a key component that produced all of the materials used in the classroom and was a pillar of the Becker organization. Also extremely important was Marketing: direct mail marketing which sent out a million pieces a year mining for the next generation of Becker students. While his salaries were competitive, the fact that he did not have a lot of high-priced executive talent, which many companies of his size would have burdened itself with, was also a great help in keeping with a lean model.

We have spoken a little about the instructors. They were broken into groups: instructors, lead instructors for the metro area, lead instructors for a multi-state territory, and national lead instructors. There were field managers who handled all of the practical aspects of each metro area. The on-site sales and marketing functions, critical toward running the business, followed the same model as the instructors, with city coordinators, area coordinators, and three national city coordinators at the top. There were also campus reps, who worked on the college campuses signing up students. Student reps, accounting majors who did some of the grunt work on campus, were not paid, but received the course for free. While the campus reps were effectively doing the outside sales work, all of these people were independent contractors working part-time. Often they were parents with younger children or people who otherwise required a flexible schedule.

NEWT AND NUTRITION

Newt was a strong proponent of good nutrition including getting your vitamins to maximize your learning capacity and your overall health. He had an almost religious belief in the value of Vitamin C and Acidophilus. As in many other areas, Newt was way ahead of his time as vitamin therapy and probiotics are now relatively common.

He also was a major advocate of getting a good night's sleep and a fair dose of exercise. He shared that with his students for two reasons. First, he felt that healthy habits were important for maximizing one's ability to take the exam. When Norm Meonske, a lead instructor, pointed out that they were still serving coffee and donuts during break time, Newt had all of the classrooms replace the donuts with apples, something that seemed to enjoy a special place in the classroom beyond its nutritional value. He included material on nutrition in the class and at Becker headquarters. Coming from a different type of personality than Newt Becker this might have been viewed as overly paternalistic and many students did see it as quirky, but people could tell that Newt cared about them. They knew if he gave advice, either in person or on tape, it was because he wanted the best for them. One Becker employee was so impressed by Newt's emphasis on healthy eating that he went on to lose a significant amount of weight during his tenure with the organization.

*Rochelle and Newt at
wedding of Rochelle's
sister Debbie (1983)*

*Rochelle and Newt
(late 1980s)*

MENTOR

Though Newt involved himself in all aspects of Becker CPA, and made all of the major and many of the minor decisions, he was always on the lookout for good people to join the organization. Once they proved themselves, he would allow them plenty of room for growth, and if they showed initiative, they could gain the kind of experience that only a growing company allows. He would also be a father figure, mentor, and friend to a good number of people, perhaps no one more than to a young man from Iran named Ramin Nadaf.

Ramin has a compelling life story. He came to the United States the year before the Islamic Revolution, finishing high school while living with a host family in Michigan. He was accepted to the University of Michigan and had gone home to update his visa. In the summer of 1979, after standing outside the U.S. Embassy for hours, he was able to get the paperwork to study in Ann Arbor. Well, he delayed and delayed, figuring he would start in January of 1980. Through a series of events so complicated they are better left for Ramin's own memoir, he was finally able to get to Ann Arbor where he earned a degree in computer science before obtaining his master's in the same discipline at Wayne State University in Detroit. Like Newt Becker, he yearned for the warm California sun, and made his way to Los Angeles where he began working at a Persian cabaret while searching for a job that would allow him to take advantage of his education and skill set.

Perusing the classified section of the *LA Times*, Ramin found a data entry position at Becker CPA, and though he may have been overqualified, he was happy when he was offered the job, and began the next day. It was 1986, and the starting pay was $6.25 an hour; Ramin kept working at the cabaret on the weekends to make ends meet. His life took an abrupt turn when he met Newt. The boss heard about Ramin's educational background and immediately bumped his pay up to $10 an hour. Then Ramin's immediate superior left for another opportunity and Newt placed Ramin in charge of the department.

There was no greater advocate of technology than Newton Becker. He was something of a student of efficiency, and realized the power of computers and programming to make his business run more efficiently and at a lower cost. Especially since he was running an operation with so many different locations and so many people working remotely, technology would allow them to coordinate their efforts in a way that would have been impossible before the advent of the personal computer. Ramin spearheaded all of the initiatives in the programming and technology areas, and Newt, who like so many of his generation was not a sophisticated user of technology, put his trust in Ramin. It was well founded and there developed between the two of them more than just trust. There was a bond that went well past the office and evolved into friendship, and even a sense of family.

Newt not only wanted his business to be fully utilizing all the available technology, he wanted to have organizations and charities that he was involved with do the same. Rather than just give them the cash to buy the much needed hardware and software, Newt would give them the technology. He would have Ramin run it just as he would any other project, finding out what they needed and determining what would work best and what could be had for the best price. AIPAC, of which Newt was a major supporter, would send Newt a wish list every couple of years of what they needed in the way of computers, printers, and the like and Ramin would handle it in his usual efficient and resourceful manner. To be involved with Newt meant you were not just in one part of his life; you were involved in many aspects of it since he was not one to compartmentalize.

Matt Aragachi came to Newt much as Ramin had. As a recent college graduate who majored in accounting, he had seen an advertisement for an entry-level accountant position and applied. He was hired and almost from the get-go came to Newt's attention. Newt could see that the young man was very talented and hardworking. He not only promoted Matt but had total trust in him. Matt had a great eye and could find where Newt's own accounting firm, and here we are speaking about the venerable Price Waterhouse, could have done things more advantageously, for example, on a tax return. He not only entrusted Matt to review the company's finances but to look at Newt's personal investments and review them for him. Again, a close relationship developed, and the two of them remained close even after Newt sold the company, after which Matt left. Matt would continue looking at Newt's investments, and the two of them would enjoy a meal or a round of golf together. Matt would go on to big things, becoming a senior financial executive for a large entertainment company based in Los Angeles.

Charles Glick, a contemporary of Matt's, was a recent graduate from UCLA with a bachelor's degree in political science. Like Matt and Ramin, Charles also answered an advertisement, this one for someone with experience in desktop publishing. Though he had never worked professionally in the field, he had plenty of experience with the software as he was the editor of the Jewish student newspaper and had been a student leader at the Westwood campus. When he interviewed with the human resources person at Becker, he was told that he lacked sufficient experience, which did not come as a total surprise to him. What did come as a total surprise was when the phone rang weeks later, and on the other end was one Newton Becker. He had seen Charles' résumé and liked what he saw. While he could not offer him the desktop publishing position, he knew he wanted to hire him and would find a job for him somewhere in the organization.

Newt found the young college graduate more than a job; he helped start him on a career path he continues to this day. Newt was a shaper of lives and gave Charles plenty of responsibility when he soon placed him in charge of the Direct Mail program. Charles, like Ramin and Matt, possessed a work ethic worthy of a man like Newton Becker, and proved to be a quick study.

As well as constantly encouraging people to work harder and smarter, Newt sought to maximize the talents of his charges. He found out what they liked and what they were good at. Charles had studied political science and was very interested in politics and public policy. When Newt formed a lobbying organization to fight the 150-Hour law (a focus of the next chapter), Newt called on Charles to head the effort. Again, Newt was not worried if someone did not have specific experience in an area. If he believed in someone, he would give that person a shot.

Ramin had come aboard in 1986, Matt and Charles four or five years later. They are just some of the many people whom Newt took under his wing who helped make the Becker organization so successful. One can surmise that Newt may have seen some of himself in all of them. They were not the first people Newt had taken chances on. In the 1970s, Newt had brought in an accountant whom he had mentored and become close to. The man had been a Jewish immigrant from the former Soviet Union and clearly had talent but just needed a chance. Newt gave him that chance and watched him rise all the way to comptroller.

It should have gone the way of the last three examples but somehow it didn't. One day Newt received a phone call from his bank. It was a bank that specialized in servicing midsize companies and Newt had a very strong relationship with his banker there. The bank had noticed that there were a number of large checks made out to MasterCard. Newt's banker had known that Newt always eschewed the use of a company credit card and was surprised to see the checks. Newt immediately knew it was trouble and headed down to the bank to look at the evidence. Sure enough, when they took a couple more steps, they determined that there had been fraud perpetrated by the comptroller. It was not a small amount, but rather well into the six figures.

While the amount was substantial, it was not the monetary loss that stung Newt the most. Though people who were around him remember that he tried to shrug the whole affair off, they also remember the pain in his eyes, the pain that comes with such an act of betrayal. What is even more surprising is that not only did Newt not prosecute the individual in question, he did not even seek civil action. Why not? The man had a daughter, and he had used the proceeds of the fraud to buy a condominium for her. Newt did not have the heart to go after it, but he did require that the comptroller pay back the theft over time. But as we will learn later, as caring and compassionate as he could be toward certain people, when it came time to fight, there was nobody more resolute.

FAMILY AND BUSINESS

The businesses that Newt was exposed to in his youth, Miller Becker and his uncle Max's bakery, were based on the model of the family bakery in Lapy, Poland. They were essentially family enterprises. While Becker CPA was not at its core a family business, there were members of the family who played critical roles in the company and it seems without question that having them in the business brought Newt a great deal of satisfaction.

It must have made Newt very happy when his brother Phil, together with his wife, Lois, came out to California upon retiring from running their children's clothing stores in the Detroit area. Newt and Phil's mother and their uncle Jack were already living in Los Angeles, and Lois, who is a cousin, also had family in California, so the move made a lot of sense.

Phil's wife, Lois, related a story that she calls "The Million Dollar Bicycle." We spoke about the tremendous impact that World War Two had on the young Newt. It was around the time he was thirteen that Newt's brother entered the U.S. Navy. Newt had wanted a new bicycle for a long time, and his brother, who had been working since he graduated from high school, had saved up money with that purpose in mind. Before he shipped out, he went to one of the biggest department stores in Cleveland and purchased the best bike he could find. Newt fell in love with that bike, for not only did it give him endless pleasure while riding it, it was practical transportation.

Newt and his brother, Phil, with their mother Rebecca (1977)

Phil would work with Newt for nearly twenty years from his arrival in California until the sale of Becker CPA to DeVry. How does the bicycle fit in? Lois felt that she and Phil, who passed away in 2010, were the beneficiaries of Newt's generosity. Phil's job, as she described it, was a cushy one; Newt had made him advertising manager, a position he thoroughly enjoyed, which allowed him to work a regular job *sans* the long hours and constant pressures that come with the retail

*Newt's brother, Phil, and Newt at party for
Newt's daughter Laura's wedding (1992)*

business. It allowed Phil and Lois to enjoy themselves as they inched toward retirement, traveling as they had not been able to do before. One million dollars doesn't begin to cover the pleasure the two brothers must have gotten from working together.

Newt would have another family member come out from the Midwest the year before his brother Phil, but it was hardly something he had planned. The sister of Newt's first wife, Sally, had passed away a number of years earlier and left three boys. As one can imagine, it was a tremendously difficult time. At nineteen years old, life is frequently filled with turmoil, even in the best of circumstances. Larry Kupps was enrolled at Ohio University, struggling with the books, and looking to make a change. Southern California looked inviting in the cold winter of 1976, and a family friend in Beachwood whom he was close to and who knew Newt, felt that Larry's uncle would help him get settled. This family friend was a good friend indeed; she got on the phone and apprised Newt of the situation. Newt had been divorced from Sally for twelve years, and having remarried and living in Los Angeles, he had not been in touch with the Kupps family. Hearing about their troubles affected him terribly. Perhaps the hardships of his own youth came to mind. Whatever the trigger, emotion turned to tears as he began to hear the story, and he told the woman that he would immediately send Larry a plane ticket and that he may move into the family's Bel Air home.

There was even more to it than just sending the ticket. Newton and Rochelle were preparing to leave for a European vacation and immediately canceled their trip. Quite amazing! After all, he could have told Larry to wait, but Newt and Rochelle realized that someone needed his help then and there, and he put his own vacation plans on hold. Having the flexibility of owning Becker CPA meant that he could put Larry to work in the office. He really took him under his wing and convinced Larry to go back to school enrolling in a local community college while working. Becker CPA turned out to be great for Larry: he gained valuable job experience; he gained confidence; and he got the chance to see Newt in action and was anxious to show his uncle he was worthy of the help he extended. Living with Newt, Rochelle, and his cousins turned out to be even better. Larry stayed in Los Angeles for enough time to gain confidence and get focused, and, after working at Becker CPA for a while, he took a job with a neighbor of Newt's who owned a large company.

Larry returned to Cleveland a changed man and became successful in the building business. Not that long after starting his own construction firm, he was on the phone with Newt one day when Newt mentioned that he was building a new classroom in one of the Becker buildings and said that he wanted Larry to do the job. Larry was reticent because the project sounded a bit more complicated than what he was used to, given the amount of paperwork required and the fact that the building was a union facility. It seemed like too many obstacles for a relatively young builder. He told his uncle that he just didn't feel he could handle the job. Newt's response was, "Of course you can do it." Sure enough, his next question was whether Larry had a fax machine, which was relatively new technology at the time. When he replied in the negative, Newt responded that he would send him one and that they could handle all the documentation without any problems. And he did. It is a great story of how Newt helped his nephew, and in many ways it illustrates what Newt was all about: helping others, reaching out, mentoring, and, most importantly, teaching—teaching others so they would be able to become independent and successful. Larry is a testament not only to Newt's goodness, but also to the importance of attaching oneself to someone who can really make a difference, a true mentor.

Rochelle's sons, Brad and Bryan, both went to work at Becker CPA. Brad spent some time there working in the direct mail area and became very good at it before leaving the firm and establishing himself in real estate. Bryan had a lengthy and successful tenure at the firm, rising, learning from Newt, and becoming assistant comptroller. When the company was sold and the position transferred to DeVry's corporate office in Chicago, Bryan stayed at the Becker CPA office in LA and went to work in information technology, further broadening his own skill set. Throughout the years Bryan became exceptionally close to Newt, working with him on his investment portfolio, the foundation, and a variety of other projects, as well as spending a lot of family time together. He is a Becker CPA graduate and still works on family business. Bryan's wife, Alison, also played a significant role in the company and no doubt this made Newt very happy. Bryan reiterated that though he would not disagree with that assessment, it was clear that Newt played no favorites and would hold his sons and other family members to the same high standards that he applied to anyone who worked at Becker, himself included. Though Newt's daughter, Laura, who was busy raising three kids, did not work there, her husband, Andy Mintzer, was a Becker instructor and is now a prominent CPA. His siblings would become Becker instructors in Florida. So there was never any shortage of family members to talk shop with.

Newt loved giving other people advice, particularly younger people, even those he had just met. As a man who saw himself primarily as an educator he would constantly extol the value of higher education. Newt received an honorary doctorate from Kent State in 1984, and his sons, David and Dan, would both earn their PhDs and go on to enjoy fine academic careers: David in neuropsychology research at the University of California, San Francisco School of Medicine and Daniel in musical composition at the San Francisco Conservatory of Music. It is hard to imagine the sense of pride this son

Newt receiving honorary doctorate from Kent State University (1984)

*Newt receiving alumnus of the year
from Kent State University (1985)*

of immigrants who was the first in his family to obtain a college degree felt when his own sons received their doctorates.

Though his interests were not in accounting, starting when he was 25, and before earning his PhD, David worked out of the Becker CPA Review Course office to create and develop an educational business called The College Success Seminar that enrolled 50,000 students during the 1980s. He used many of Newt's approaches in marketing, administration, and audio-visual educational materials, which gave Newt great satisfaction. Years later, David became involved in the charitable foundation, and, at age 50, left his academic career at UCSF to join his father and run it, which you will hear a good deal more about later in this book.

Dan's experiences directing an academic department and his common bond with his father as a fellow educator led to many conversations that encompassed Newt's experiences at Becker and with his philanthropies.

If educating and mentoring people and family members involved with the business brought great joy to Newton Becker, there were areas of running Becker CPA that brought him great aggravation as well. Running the company was like life itself, chock-full of challenges as the business matured. Becker's status as an industry leader was to make it a target, not only of its many competitors, but sadly, of a misguided lawsuit brought about by the United States Department of Justice.

CHAPTER FIVE

Becker CPA's Challenges and Legacy

NEWT AND THE AMERICANS WITH DISABILITIES ACT

"I know that there may be concerns that the ADA may be too vague or too costly, or may lead endlessly to litigation. But I want to reassure you right now that my administration and the United States Congress have carefully crafted this Act. We've all been determined to ensure that it gives flexibility, particularly in terms of the timetable of the implementation; and we've been committed to containing the costs that may be incurred. . . ."

These were the words spoken by George H. W. Bush after signing the Americans with Disabilities Act (ADA) of 1990,

111

perhaps the most famous piece of legislation associated with his presidency. Unfortunately, the Americans with Disabilities Act *did* turn out to be very vague and very costly, and it led to plenty of litigation, although our concern here is the 1993 case known as *The United States of America v. Becker CPA Review, Ltd.,* which had the dubious distinction of being the first case filed by the Justice Department to enforce the ADA.

The ADA legislation, like so many grand legislative initiatives of its kind, grew out of good intentions. The intention was to increase accessibility for people with disabilities, allowing them to participate fully in American social, educational, cultural, and commercial life. The legislation forced builders to construct their edifices in such a way as to accommodate those with handicaps, mandated parking lot owners to have the requisite number of handicapped parking spaces, and required of schools and other institutions, whether public or private, a set of policies that facilitated the use of their services, of whatever nature, to those with handicaps.

Dr. Norman Meonske, Becker CPA's lead instructor in Akron and a professor of accounting at Newt's alma mater, Kent State University, recalls that he heard about the Federal lawsuit against Becker on the radio. He couldn't believe it. "Newt had advised us long before the ADA legislation to always accommodate students with special needs."

One of the primary disabilities is hearing impairment. Becker CPA had over the years accommodated at least ten such students in a variety of ways. The primary aid was to provide students with written transcripts from the tapes, including written recommended instructor interjects for the live instructor, and to sit the students—if they read lips—next to the instructor. There was nary a complaint, that is, until a student in Washington, DC requested a sign language interpreter. Newt did not believe that an interpreter would help much and believed that the accommodations that Becker had already made were what the law called for, that is, "reasonable modifications." When asked about the necessity of an interpreter, one of his deaf students responded this way in an *LA Times* article about the case: "No, no no!" he said in a phone interview from his home with his wife relaying the questions. "It's not the interpreter. Becker provided everything I needed. The key to passing is doing the homework." But the deaf student in Washington, DC felt differently and took it to the Department of Justice, which had enforcement responsibility for the legislation.

The student had attended sessions for the first two weeks and had yet to pay for the course. Becker CPA allowed all students to take two weeks' worth of classes before paying for them. It is a further testament to Newt's focus on the student. He did not want to take a dime from anyone who did not feel he was were getting the appropriate value for his money, which was significant, and Newt was convinced that the quality of the course would sell itself—which it did. Newt had argued that in addition to the unproven aspect of an interpreter helping, the price of the interpreter was over three times the amount of the tuition paid by the student, a factor that will figure later in our discussion. The government, however, did not even seek to work on a resolution to a conflict over a law that had just been enacted and pursued legal action. A case was filed within a month of the student's complaint.

Though he sympathized with the student's predicament, Newt felt his lower-cost remedy was adequate. The student in question obviously felt it was not, and concluded this on the basis that his wife, who was a trained sign translator, had come to one of the classes to interpret for him—which Becker had gladly allowed—and that she had helped him. Why he felt that Becker should provide this help goes back to the crux of the case and the ADA legislation.

The government claimed that Becker had not adequately changed its policies to comply with the legislation, and even when it tried to, whatever changes it came up with were inadequate. The government aggressively proceeded with its case, hoping to impose both a remedy and damages. Newt diligently fought the case, though, given the legal fees and the aggravation that followed, a *mea culpa* would have cost less—both economically and emotionally.

Another aspect of this points to the personality of Newt as well. Newt was a highly determined and tenacious champion of a cause. In this case, while agreeing with the general intent of the ADA, he felt that the way it was being interpreted was ridiculously overreaching. He felt it was unjust and unreasonable for the government to require a tremendously expensive interpreter (up to $9,000 in 1992) who provided minimal benefit at a cost that not only eliminated the $1,300 tuition from this student, but that could put him up to $7,700 in the hole for each student. He thought it was reasonable for government agencies to adopt these standards for their own operations, but unreasonable to impose them on private businesses.

In addition to feeling that he had made a reasonable modification and had not violated the law, Newt justified his confrontational stance because he understood that while he could afford to make accommodations, whether reasonable or not, there were plenty of smaller companies that could not. That

*Brad, Bryan, Newt, David, Laura & Rochelle
at Bryan's wedding (1988)*

was typical Newt, and again it goes back to feeling for the underdog, even though by now he was sufficiently successful no longer to qualify as such.

The only problem with fighting the government is that it has unlimited resources with which to do battle. Eventually Newt decided to cut his losses and move on. In the end, a settlement was reached, and Newt established a scholarship for deaf students in accounting as well as agreeing to policy changes. The pain and aggravation were more expensive than the legal costs. For such a good guy to be painted in a negative light surely had to have hurt. It must have annoyed Newt to have himself portrayed unsympathetically in an article that appeared in the *Los Angeles Times*.

There is something else to be said about this episode. More than anything, Newt cared deeply about all of his students. He had initiated the practice of being at the test site on test day to wish them well and pass out "good luck" apples—a practice that his instructors would continue. He had tutored them on how to take the test, on what to eat, and on the importance of a good night's sleep. At first, he would call his students himself to find out how they did. Later as the organization grew, his instructors and staff would do the same.

Newt worked hard to learn everyone's name in the class and would then go around the room to introduce each person and the name of his firm (even if there were 80 students in a class!). Newt was known to sit in bed and memorize the many names by comparing a photo of the whole class with the sign in sheet that had been passed from row to row. He extended himself in this very personal way and it endeared him to his many students.

Providing they had attended the sessions and done their homework, students could re-take the course gratis if they did not pass. He established a bond with students from the first day they met him or heard his voice. It was a bond that often lasted for years. Newt built their self-confidence and as long as they knew he was in their corner, the dreaded exam seemed passable. This episode with the ADA seemed to be the only negative experience that Newt ever endured from a student, a real anomaly in the history of Becker CPA. Perhaps there were other students who presented serious problems for Newt, but, if so, you would have a hard time finding them. Whereas even the judge who had heard the case felt that the Justice Department had overreached, and so many, including many of his competitors, were sympathetic, the whole episode was a bitter one—though it did not embitter him as much as it might have a lesser man.

CARE CPA

Newt had his hands full in the early 1990s. Not only did he have to deal with the Federal Government regarding the ADA, but he had to spend a good portion of his time dealing with state governments as well. This was in reaction to legislation that had been proposed in state legislatures throughout the country. It was called the 150-Hour Law, and it threatened not only to hurt the Becker business, but to change the accounting profession substantially.

What was the 150-Hour Law? The law required 150 hours of college work in order to sit for the CPA exam. This effectively amounts to a fifth year of college work. While requiring

Newt & Rochelle at their 20th wedding anniversary party (1991)

another degree in addition to a bachelor's degree had been a topic of discussion going back into the 1950s, it was only in 1979 that any state had enacted such a law. That was in the Sunshine State, and, as one can imagine, it was done primarily to protect longtime Florida CPAs against encroachments from those who were CPAs in other states but had come to escape the winter weather of their home states, or retirees who wished to continue practicing.

Who was behind the 150-Hour Law, and what did he hope to accomplish with its passing? To understand this, we need to know a little bit about the accounting profession. According to the Merriam-Webster dictionary, a profession is defined as "a calling requiring specialized knowledge and often long and intensive academic preparation." While the word *profession* is often used loosely, three professions that are at the top of most lists are the medical, legal, and accounting professions. Medicine generally requires four years of post-baccalaureate work, law requires three extra years, but accounting required only an undergraduate degree to sit for the CPA exam.

Some in the accounting profession had long felt that it lacked status in comparison to other professions. Not only did very few accounting professionals have master's degrees in accounting, but most of the schools of accounting were located within larger business schools. There was a great desire to build independent schools of accountancy and the big firms (they started as the Big Eight and eventually consolidated to the Big Four) were taking steps to help establish them.

In addition, there were pressures put on the industry and its membership organization responsible for the profession's ethical code. Significant scandals and frauds beginning with the Savings and Loan Crisis in the 1980s created governmental pressure to increase regulation and oversight of the industry. A 150-Hour Law could be pointed to in the industry as something that was being done to improve standards and ethics by increasing educational requirements.

There is something peculiar about the choice of a 150-Hour Law. If there was going to be an additional requirement for licensing, then a master's degree or 180 hours would have been the logical choice. A requirement of a two-year master's degree was rejected as being too onerous, so requiring 150 hours was seen as a compromise. What made the rule even stranger was that the additional 30 hours did not necessarily have to be in accounting. One guide that this writer found toward obtaining the CPA recommends that students take courses at a local community college in order to lessen the cost. This whole approach for 150 hours seemed, for a field that was so logical and practical, to lack both characteristics.

Until 1989, only Florida, Tennessee, and Utah had enacted legislation requiring the 150 hours. The big change occurred in 1989 when the American Institute of Certified Public Accountants (AICPA) officially endorsed the idea and began actively working toward its passage through lobbying the individual state legislatures.

Norm Meonske, Newt's friend and lead instructor in Akron, became aware of impending legislation in Ohio. He immediately set out to oppose the 150-Hour Law. He felt that the reasons given for its passage by the AICPA, the big firms, and certain figures in academia were either faulty or self-serving. Norm seemed to agree with Newt whom he said called the law "the CPA-ego enhancement and full employment of graduate faculty act." Norm began speaking out against it at professional and academic meetings and made its defeat as big a

At wedding party for Newt's niece (1992)

cause célèbre as anything that the accounting profession had ever seen. Eventually, he would debate anyone at any college campus or association meeting from the other side.

One might think that Norm, as an academic, might favor the legislation as a way of being able to teach many more hours, assuming that at least some of the additional thirty hours would be taken in the undergraduate school in accounting. He rightly saw that it would not increase the number of class hours for accounting professors, but that it would turn students away from majoring in accounting. Perhaps the greatest attraction of the field was its practical nature—one could reasonably expect to be able to work with no additional requirements once one graduated. Many students coming from middle and lower income families saw the CPA profession as the shortest route to membership in the professional class.

There was a personal side of this for Norm. If Newt's class background was limited, then Norm's was positively trying. He grew up in Wichita, and for a while lived above a store and did not actually have a physical address. He worked in a grocery store as a carry-out boy to help his parents put groceries on their table, and though he was a good student in high school, he did not imagine going beyond his high school diploma. It was only through the kindly intervention of a professor at Wichita State University, who was a customer at the grocery store, that Norm found himself in college. He would end up obtaining not only his undergraduate degree in accounting, but continued on for a PhD. Despite his considerable professional success, like Newt, he never lost touch with his roots, and he realized what the requirement of 150 hours would do to students with limited financial resources.

As a Becker instructor who was in constant touch with Newt, he alerted Newt as to what was going on in Ohio. At first, Newt, perhaps preoccupied with other matters, did not take an active interest in the upcoming legislation. But as several states passed laws in 1990, Newt realized that he was the logical person to fight the 150-Hour Law, and took up the mantle with his usual gusto.

If Florida was any indication of how the passage of such legislation could change things, then the law was going to be a serious problem for Becker CPA. In 1983, the year before Florida's law became effective, 3,294 accountants took the test for the first time. In 1984, those taking it for the first time dropped to 54. Naturally, the four-year period between enacted and effective was largely to blame for such a precipitous drop. But if fewer people took the CPA exam because of the new requirement, and Becker's business depended on maximizing the number of students taking the exam, then the law presented a serious challenge to Newt.

Based on discussions with Norm, the two came to the conclusion that the only course of action was to form an organization that would fight the impending legislation. They came up with a name, the Coalition Against Restrictive Entry into the CPA profession, which had the advantage of a clever acronym, CARE CPA. Newt would use his Becker offices, hire an executive director, and together with Norm, who was waging his own battle, got busy.

The term *coalition* implies that you have other people working on your side. The obvious allies were those who would be most hurt by the law, and those most vulnerable to it were ethnic and racial minorities. The National Council of Philippine-American Certified Public Accountants was one of the first to come aboard and actively oppose the legislation. The Hispanic Coalition on Higher Education and assorted Asian CPA firms, largely composed of immigrants or children of immigrants, came aboard. Various Mexican-American groups, particularly powerful in California, actively opposed it. The Association of Community and Junior Colleges, whose student body strongly represented those from limited economic circumstances that we mentioned, weighed in strongly against it. There were others who strongly opposed the 150-Hour Law, too, such as William H. Reed who was the director of the Defense Contract Audit Agency supervising thousands of CPAs. But most important was getting the African-American community behind the efforts of CARE CPA. The National Association of Black

Accountants had come out against the law, as had the Council of Minority Business Organizations, as well as the Office for the Advancement of Public Black Colleges. All of this was very positive, but in the early 1990s there was one man whose support was critical. This man was the one person whom even the greatest titans of American business were loathe to offend. It was hoped that Rick Elam, then vice president for Education for the AICPA and who was spearheading the efforts to pass the law, would feel the same way.

Jesse Jackson and Newton Becker were pretty unlikely allies, but the cause was worthy, and Newt was all for pursuing the African-American man who had been a presidential candidate in two elections, as well as the head of Operation Push and the Rainbow Coalition. Charles Glick, who had taken over as executive director of CARE CPA, pursued the charismatic leader with dogged determination and finally caught up with him as he was about to enter his limousine after a speaking engagement. He had only a minute to make his pitch, and it must have been successful because Rev. Jackson provided him with the name of someone in the National Rainbow Coalition with whom to coordinate efforts. Ultimately, a letter was written under the letterhead of the National Rainbow Coalition. When reading it, it is fairly obvious that it was not written by the man who signed it, or anyone at the Rainbow Coalition, as it clearly and concisely presented the position of CARE CPA.

Jackson's support lent strength to the cause, particularly in the African-American community, which was badly underrepresented in the profession. Editorials followed in major African-American newspapers. An article about Jackson's support followed in *Accounting Today*, a major trade publication.

What was accomplished by all of the efforts of CARE CPA? Considering that the effort lasted only a few years and was done on a shoestring budget, particularly in comparison to what the AICPA could throw at the effort for the other side, one would have to say a great deal.

One of the greatest successes was that CARE CPA bought time. Delaware did not enact a law until 2008. California, Becker's home territory, after several failed attempts, finally passed the law in 2009, and the last holdout, Colorado, came aboard in 2010, 21 years after the AICPA officially endorsed the 150-Hour Law. But the success was more than just a delaying action. They were able to play a role in getting a provision put through in many of the states that somewhat ameliorated the effect of the law. It allowed students to take the exam after 120 hours, though they would not be licensed until they reached the 150-hour requirement. There were proposals in other states to lower the experience requirement from two years to one year, or to substitute experience for the education. Perhaps more than anything, CARE CPA won some battles but ultimately lost the war, as the 150-hour law increasingly became seen as a fait accompli. While Newt was not unrealistic—delaying passage of this law was clearly beneficial to Becker CPA—he did not easily concede defeat. He felt the 150-Hour Law was bad for the accounting profession and for his business and he fought it for as long as he could.

Between 1989 and 1995, twenty-six states enacted 150-Hour Laws. The laws, however, would not become effective until five to ten years after they were enacted. So in 1991, the most students in the history of the CPA exam took the test—140,000. Newt realized that this number would surely decrease; the only question was by how much? While he may have been better positioned than his smaller competitors to absorb a downturn, it was possible to see that by the end of the decade, business would go down.

There were other factors that were cause for worry by 1995. There had been an explosion in the field of computers, and the high-tech boom, buoyed by monumental growth in telecommunications and the soon-to-be Internet start-ups, were increasing demand for professionals in all of these fields. The thought was that computers would attract some of the same types who had been drawn to accounting. Another concern in the 1990s was that some of the corporate scandals portrayed the accounting profession in a negative light. Those scandals would get worse in the next decade or so with Enron, WorldCom, and other accounting based debacles. Suffice it to say, there were big challenges to the profession. While Newt must have felt vindicated in emphasizing professional ethics in his review course, he must have fretted somewhat about the future of the field.

Another factor may have even figured in slightly. As computer technology was getting increasingly more sophisticated and more interactive, there would have to be changes in all of the Becker CPA Review audio-visual materials to adapt to this changing marketplace. Those changes, which were already being implemented by a competitor, were necessary but time-consuming and costly. Newt's competitors, as we discussed in the previous chapter, were increasingly more formidable in a variety of ways.

DEVRY

In 1996, Newt was two years away from his seventieth birthday. Due to all of the reasons mentioned above, he must have been thinking what Becker CPA would look like in the coming millennium. Though Newt had mentored so many people, he had never groomed anyone to take over for him. It is doubtful that anyone really could have taken his place. He gave people projects to run with, accompanied by his famous directive, "I want you to pilot this," so while he may have delegated certain responsibilities, he did not divide decision making. He was as they say "a force of one."

At one point Newt brought in a management consultant to make some changes. While the consultant stayed around for a few years trying to change the organizational chart and presumably spearhead some actual organizational changes, in the end the initiative went nowhere. Newt was plenty happy with his and Becker's modus operandi for the two were the same. He never brought in anyone from the outside at a senior level with thoughts of succession. His philanthropic endeavors had always been most important, and as we will discuss in the following chapter, he was also heavily involved in Luz and other investments during the time he was running Becker. Miraculously, somehow he managed to balance it all, but it seemed time to begin to slow down and he knew that his commitments to Becker, outside investments, and philanthropic involvements would make for a more difficult balancing act in the future.

As it turned out, Newt made the decision to sell and began to look for an appropriate buyer. There were not too many logical choices. He was the big player in the market, so selling to a competitor was out of the question. Newt engaged an investment banker, Michael Kane, whom his stockbroker and friend David Pollock had recommended, to handle all of the tasks involved in putting a company for sale. The logical choice was a big for-profit educational company, one that could easily absorb Becker. It was determined that DeVry Inc. was a good candidate, and it was.

Headquartered in Chicago, DeVry began as a technical institute in 1931 and was an early entrant into that field. A controlling interest was purchased by Chicago-based Bell and Howell in 1966. The innovative maker of motion picture cameras and other technology had long had an education division, and it expanded the division in the following two decades. Growth had slowed in the mid-1980s, and Bell and Howell decided to sell its interest in DeVry to two former employees, Dennis Keller and Ron Taylor.

Keller and Taylor originally met at DeVry where Taylor was a controller and Keller had toiled in marketing as a newly minted MBA. They decided to strike out on their own in 1973, with very ambitious plans to create a new model of a business school, one that would be run like the subject matter it taught—as a business. Known today as Keller Graduate School, the founders were part of a real start-up story, and, despite long odds, like Newt Becker, they got their big break in 1977 when the school received accreditation.

Their niche was in appealing to older students who needed a more flexible schedule in order to take courses, and needed campuses close by long before traditional universities began to be sensitive to working professionals and nontraditional students—a sensitivity they would act on after acquiring their old employer.

They had ideas on how to run DeVry, and how to complement it with business training, which was their specialty. With only 4 million dollars in sales, they bought DeVry for 182 million dollars in 1987. They took DeVry's name, which was far better known than their own, and began running a large enterprise appealing to the new demand for high technology that DeVry could offer. Because they were growth oriented and hardly risk averse, Becker CPA Review was very appealing.

Their reasons were obvious. First, they were financial buyers, and they were looking for an acquisition that would strengthen their firm's long-term financial prospects. Next, there was a further appeal on the basis of increasing the prestige and reputation of DeVry. For-profit private education had long suffered from a lack of status compared to its nonprofit public and private cousins. It met an important need, initially in technical and vocational education and later in undergraduate and graduate programs, but was largely suspect. Becker CPA Review, though it was also a for-profit operation, had a sterling reputation and would only enhance the DeVry name. Last, from a strategic point of view, there was the benefit of incorporating Becker into its educational offerings which would attract accounting students and substantially add to DeVry's enrollment. All in all, it seemed like a good fit.

Newt, of course, wanted to make sure that DeVry would continue to run the course—at least in terms of its most important dimension, the course content—in the same manner in which he had run it. They then agreed on the price. Newt planned to give the majority of the proceeds to his foundation. To help facilitate that, Newt had transferred ownership of Becker CPA to the Newton D. Becker and Rochelle F. Becker Foundation, which is a Jewish community foundation you will hear a good deal about later. Suffice it to say, it reflects Newt's values that the ultimate beneficiary of his vision would not be himself or his family, but rather his philanthropy.

The deal was signed in June 1996, 37 years after Newt taught his first formal course to a group of 10 students. During that time, Newt had helped about 200,000 students pass the

CPA Exam in 143 cities, including eight cities in foreign countries. Becker CPA Review Course's passing rate was nearly
double the national average of 30 percent and nearly 40 percent of all people passing the CPA Exam were Becker students.

Newt would stay on for two years during a transitional
period, and, of course, would still loom mightily as a figure-
head even after his formal involvement ended, as he does still
today even after his death. It is never easy when a founder,
no less than a man with the gravitas of a Newton Becker, sells
his company. Employees who initially remained in place had
a difficult adjustment as they went from working for Newt to
working for a large company.

The instructors did their best to acclimate and most
stayed, accepting whatever changes in policies DeVry instituted. Norm Meonske is still teaching for Becker, as are several
longtime instructors. One of the most important figures who
has remained for over twenty-six years now is Newt's protégée and close friend, Ramin Nadaf. Ramin ran information
technology, but, because of family commitments and harsh
winters, declined to relocate to DeVry's corporate headquarters in Chicago. Instead, he kept a strong contingent of people
in the Encino branch where he is a vice president and is in
charge of course content, a development that made Newt very
happy and assured him that his legacy would remain intact.

That is not to say there was no conflict with DeVry. A man
with Newt's singular approach to doing things could not avoid
conflict, particularly when changes that he disagreed with
were made and he was largely powerless to prevent them.
That is not to say that the management of what became a
division of DeVry known as Becker Professional Education
did not listen to Newt. Tom Vucinic, who would go on to run

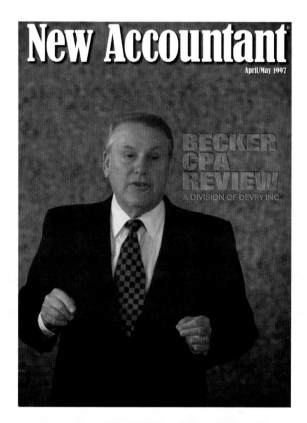

Newt on the cover of the April/May 1997 issue of
New Accountant featuring an article about Becker CPA's
"new partnership with Devry, Inc."

the division, spoke about a time when Newt was visiting the corporate headquarters. As he recalled, "a crowd had gathered around Newt as if he was Robert Redford." Tom Vucinic remembers an industry convention that the two attended together in which they had spent several hours together

Becker CPA Review

Poised for A New Era of Growth

As we head toward the 21st century, Becker CPA Review has never been more optimistic about its future and the opportunities for growth. An expanding, globalized economy and the worldwide acceptance of the U.S. CPA designation has opened the door for CPA review courses to expand internationally. Leading-edge technology allows us to deliver our programs through new media to new audiences. And our new partnership with DeVry Inc. provides us with valuable new resources and opportunities that will greatly benefit our students.

As the acknowledged industry leader in our field, Becker CPA Review prepares students to take the nationally administered Certified Public Accountant (CPA) and the Certified Management Accountant (CMA) exams. With more than 210,000 CPA alumni, the review course is offered in more than 140 U.S. cities and 16 international markets.

Through our alliance with DeVry Inc., which includes DeVry Institutes and Keller Graduate School of Management, we will not only maintain our competitive strength, but widen the scope of accounting-related educational services available to students.

Before we discuss the future, let's go back to the very beginning.

Filling a Need

Becker CPA Review got its start in response to my own personal need. In 1956, I was working on a master's degree at Case Western Reserve University and had just about completed three years of employment with Price Waterhouse in Cleveland. At that time in Ohio, three years of work experience were required before sitting for the CPA exam.

BY NEWTON D. BECKER, CPA - FOUNDER AND DIRECTOR OF BECKER CPA REVIEW

Opening pages of the article about Becker CPA Review

walking around the inside perimeter of the hotel, with Newt regaling Tom with stories about the business, not just to entertain though surely he did, but to emphasize certain important points about Becker CPA.

Speaking with Newt several months before his passing, he spoke well of DeVry and felt that he had made the right decision in selling to it. He was amazed at how it had been able to expand the business. An important event was held in 2007, the fiftieth anniversary of the founding of Becker. The founding dates back to 1957, when Newt first began teaching his colleagues at Price Waterhouse. In 1999, DeVry had acquired Becker's biggest competitor, Conviser Miller Duffy. They renamed the division Becker Conviser CPA, but at the fiftieth anniversary party, it was announced that the name would go back to Becker CPA for as long as DeVry had anything to say about it.

Newt's response was very un-Newt-like. He was moved to tears. These were clearly tears of pride, but one wonders if there was not a pinch of sadness mixed in because he was no longer involved. It was an extraordinary achievement: a real golden anniversary. Yet the real celebrants were not the instructors, employees, DeVry executives, or even Newt himself. They were the legions of former Becker students, at that point estimated at 400,000—about half of all the CPAs in the country—whose lives had been changed thanks to Newt. It is no wonder that he was proud of that legacy, but as you will read ahead, it is only one part of a much larger one.

CHAPTER SIX

Solar Energy and Israeli Bioengineering

I think the future for solar energy is bright.
—Ken Salazar, U.S. Secretary of the Interior, 2011

Solar power is clean, renewable and cost effective but it also takes time to develop.
—J. D. Hayworth, U.S. Congressman, 2006

LUZ

It is hard to believe but when Newton Becker first became chairman of the world's largest solar energy company, Ken Salazar, now a grandfather and the current Secretary of the Interior, was still in law school, and J. D. Hayworth, former congressman, was donning cap and gown to receive his baccalaureate. It seems so unlikely a story that an accountant, the founder of a group of schools that prepare students for the CPA exam, would one day be described as an alternative energy maven and "the father of the solar thermal electric generation."

How did it all happen? Irwin Field, Newt's friend, fellow philanthropist and fellow investor introduced him to a gentleman named Arnold Goldman who was looking to raise money for a company with the name of Luz that he had formed with a Frenchman named Patrick Francois. Goldman was trained as an electrical engineer and like so many engineers, he worked for a large defense contractor in Southern California before leaving to start a stand-alone word processor company in the early years of computers. Goldman, who seemed to possess a brilliant and highly innovative mind, cashed out on his technology by selling the company to Raytheon Corporation, and moved to Jerusalem in the mid-1970s.

With time on his hands, Goldman set out to write a book called *A Working Paper on Project Luz*. Luz was named after the biblical location of Jacob's ladder that connected heaven and earth. Not one to harp on the small stuff, Goldman focused his efforts on weighty material like the meaning of life and how to save the world. As has been reported in a number of periodicals and books, Goldman fused together ideas about science, philosophy, and religion. Born in Providence, Rhode Island, perhaps Goldman felt connected with the New England Transcendentalists and weighed in with his own version of Utopia. While not the rustic beauty of Walden Pond, Luz was a model city or series of cities that Goldman planned to build, a communitarian and economic vision not yet seen. The city was to be powered by the sun and Goldman actually planned on building cities based on this model. It was far more complicated than that as John Berger points out in his book on renewable energy, *Charging Ahead*, where he explains Goldman's esoteric vision:

> *"Goldman envisioned Luz as 12 component communities surrounded by an appealing yet functional wall composed "of a long series of parabolas which focus light on an energy-absorption tube," so as to gather much of the energy the community would need. Two major industries would contribute to the city's economy. The first was a Solar Modular Housing Corporation that was to produce kits enabling families to design and build their own environmentally sound homes. The second was to be an International Solar Equipment Corporation that would produce solar energy-generation equipment.*
>
> *For Goldman, part of this systematic philosophical thought was to test the validity of his ideas in the real world. When he finished his book in 1979, he decided that a business environment would be the most challenging place to explore the "integrative understandings" he had developed. So in 1979, he started a company called Independent Household Products (IHP).*
>
> *Goldman initially saw IHP as a city-building company and began searching for investors. Financiers, however, were not persuaded when he talked to them about the new firm. The project was too large and difficult for them to grasp and would have required massive funding."*

One can certainly sympathize with those investors, and can almost imagine that after hearing the whole spiel they may have remarked with the classic line, "From this you make a living?" While Goldman still believed in the totality of his vision, there were practical considerations at work, even for a visionary. He toned down the enterprise to focus on building a solar energy company.

There were reasons on Goldman's part to feel that the time was right for a serious solar company, and one that did business in the United States, which was to become the venue for his company's activities. The year of its founding, 1979, featured the second energy crisis on U.S. soil in less than six years, and as someone once remarked, "You never want to let a crisis go to waste."

The first crisis had been a result of the 1973 Yom Kippur War when OPEC and the Arab oil-producing countries decided to punish the United States for its support of Israel by placing an embargo on the United States that led to a tightening of the oil supply and a spike in its prices. This, in turn, led to long lines at the gas pump as conservation methods were instituted. The second crisis was related to the events that surrounded the fall of the Shah of Iran and the ensuing tumult in that oil-rich nation. Cheap oil looked to be a thing of the past.

There were some good signs, however. The environmental movement was nearing the end of its first decade and was becoming more and more mainstream. Among the chief villains of the movement were the big polluters of which fossil fuel use figured heavily. The atmosphere in Washington for alternative energy seemed to be right. Jimmy Carter, elected a few years earlier in 1976, was more than just a peanut farmer. An Annapolis graduate, he had a background in nuclear engineering and had created a new cabinet-level federal agency, the Department of Energy. When it came to oil, he may have liked the peanut variety, but he was a major fan of green energy and had increased funding in research and develop-ment toward developing a full spectrum of alternatives to fos-sil fuels. In practicing what he preached he had installed solar panels at the White House.

Goldman did not have a product, a market, or even a prototype, just a 2½ foot model of a solar collector trough to show Newt Becker when the two met in December 1979, yet it appears that Newt was almost immediately sold on the idea. As he was right in the middle of his tenure in running Becker CPA, the question is why did Newt want to take on this quixotic venture? Even if he did want to be an investor, why take on the chairmanship of the holding company? Why? Newt Becker might respond, "Why not?" As Bryan Gordon so astutely points out, this is what made Newt go. This was the fuel that he ran on. David Becker puts forward five reasons that best explain Newt's attraction to Luz:

1. The opportunity to make a huge impact and to change the world for the better in a critical and profound way. Newt was very excited about this incredible opportunity to make history and believed that he had the skills, resources, and determina-tion to make this happen. He fully recognized the importance of ushering in the solar era, and now that the path ahead was clear to him, he may have also felt the responsibility of being the right man in the right place at the right time.

2. Reducing the global power of Arab oil. The Arab Oil Embargo of 1973, related to the Yom Kippur War when Arab countries launched a surprise attack on Israel, highlighted the vulnerability of the West to the use of Arab oil as a weapon. A second oil crisis in 1979 was fresh on everyone's mind when

Newt met Arnold Goldman in December 1979. If you could lessen dependency on OPEC, that would be good for both America and Israel—and everyone else except OPEC and the Arab states.

3. Environmental concerns. If you could increase the use of renewable energy, and lessen the use of the polluting fossil fuels, that would be good for the entire planet. It just made so much sense—the earth was running out of fossil fuels and this would provide clean, and eventually cheap, energy for the future. Newt may have been an environmentalist of a different stripe from the type one normally encounters, but in his own way he was very much both environmentalist and conservationist.

4. The challenge of it all. As Irwin Field pointed out earlier, Newt loved a project that he could get his teeth into. Whether it was designing a hardtop for a convertible, or creating a solar energy industry, Newt was never put off by the challenges of a project. If he felt it was the right thing to do, he wanted to do it all the more. Newt seemed to subscribe to that ageless American mantra that has been adopted by the U.S. Armed Forces, "The difficult we do today, the impossible takes a little longer," and *impossible* is not a bad word to describe what faced Luz.

5. Return on investment. You may have noticed that last on the list was the return on investment, or the dollars that would flow to the investor, presumably the most important consideration for most of them. That, of course is precisely the point. To Newton Becker, the four items outlined above *were* the return on investment. Ah, but what of financial return, you ask, since he was, after all, planning on sinking a considerable amount of his own cash in this Luz enterprise. Newt believed that Luz could return a handsome dividend to investors. No matter how much Newt may have been out to change the world and been attracted to the reasons above, he also felt this was a very real money making opportunity. But it seems clear that money was not what drove him. He was, after all, out to change the world.

Luz was able to raise significant amounts of money in its early round of financing and assembled a top-flight technology team to develop a prototype to show investors. As all seemed to agree, the short period that it took to develop the prototype was exceptional and they were able to go back to investors for a second round of financing. Though Goldman and his partner had put some of their own money into the start-up, by far, the largest investor was, as you might have guessed, Newt.

Newt brought more than his money. He brought his enthusiasm, determination, financial acumen, and his accountant's eye for detail as well as a practical, pragmatic engineer's approach. He also had the ability to grasp science and technology and explain it to fellow investors. Newt would really need to apply all of his talent; as the challenges were great, and solar would have to be price competitive with fossil fuels, Luz would need every bit of it.

Given that so much of what Luz was taking on was essentially new territory, it was never clear what would work. To make solar power you needed a solar collector to gather the rays of the sun, and the pioneers at Luz tried theirs out on a kibbutz in Israel. Success followed, and now they needed real customers. The initial thought was to use solar to power industrial systems for the large textile manufacturers located in the

Southeastern United States. They did get several on board, but could never get the critical mass that was needed to make the venture profitable. The Southeast turned out to be less than ideal for solar. As John Berger points out in his book, and he conducted extensive interviews with Newt, the ideal solar conditions were to be found in the deserts of Southern California and the Southwest. Of course, that was not where these manufacturers were located, so as Berger points out, "At first Becker did not want to accept the conclusion that there was no future for Luz in industrial-process steam. He and Goldman tried selling systems to hospitals and other possible customers. 'We squandered two million dollars,' Becker recalls. As the process-heat initiative fizzled, the company ran out of money. 'We had to lay off that whole sales force,' said Becker. 'We cut back the company dramatically.'"

Luz' offices were now in the Becker CPA Review Course office suite, and they had to find a new market and find it quickly. Newt involved himself in the nitty-gritty of the operation just as he did at Becker CPA. That he was able to do this, in a field that he essentially had no experience in, simply boggles the mind. Despite the stress, the challenge of figuring it all out seemed to excite Newt. As this excerpt from Berger amply illustrates, there were myriad technical challenges—this one relates to the solar collector—and Newt was right in the thick of it.

> *Besides the early heat losses, another significant problem was the massive bulk of the solar collector. "It was like a tank," Newton Becker said. "You needed a crane to move a three-foot section." This led to huge fabrication and shipping costs. Becker was not the kind of investor willing to sit back and let his money dissipate, however. Becker*

the financier put on an engineer's hat and drew a more elegant solar-collector design. The new module would use molded glass that could support its own weight and therefore would require a much less massive frame and could be shipped economically in stacks. The new collector could be built for a fraction of its predecessor's cost.

The story is filled with many crucial details, but in the end Luz would be building solar plants that would provide electricity for Southern California Edison. While the land for the facility was given to them by the utility, the cost for building the plant would be borne by Luz.

The financing was in place, with a prime investment banking firm raising the $40 million needed. Bad news came in the form of the discovery that $40 million would not be enough to get the job done. They needed $60 million to capture the heat of the sun. The financial institution, put off by the 50 percent increase, backed out and now Newt needed to come up with the additional money, or fold his hand.

Newt and Luz were able to get the money. For the investment to be profitable, it needed the federal investment credits as well as California tax credits. There was great pressure because the tax credits expired at the end of 1984 and the plant had to be online in the same calendar year as it was built. So if SEGS I (Solar Electric Generating System I) was not operational by New Year's Eve, the investors were out of luck. The biggest risk, and the investor stood to lose everything, was if the technology simply did not work. Fortunately, it did.

Between 1984 and 1990, Luz built nine plants for over a billion dollars collectively. Investors who financed the stations made money, the stations themselves worked well, and, at the time, those nine plants produced 90 percent of the world's solar electrical energy. They are still in use today. But the great dream that Arnold Goldman brought to Newt and others took a bad turn, and, in 1991, twelve years after Newt first met Arnold Goldman, the company went bankrupt. What happened?

The financial model that led to profitability for investors, and therefore the ability to build plants, was based on tax credits. During the 1980s these had to be renewed by Congress each year. Luz was by far the largest solar company operating, and as Scott Sklar, the industry's major lobbyist at the time, explained, it meant that Newt and Arnold Goldman were in his DC office, sometimes as often as every two weeks. They were lobbying constantly, and it was a monumental struggle. In 1990, Congress extended the credits to only nine months rather than a full year, which meant the plants would have to be online before October 1st.

Newt was understandably frustrated by this, as what he really needed was permanent, or at least multi-year, tax credits. This would have been enough to deal with, but, in addition to Washington, the focus was also on Sacramento. Luz depended on a continuing property tax exemption, but a new governor, who was misinformed by his finance department, initially vetoed an extension of the exemption. Although the extension was later approved, this delay essentially killed the final plant because one of the major financiers pulled out in the interim. With this delay, the plant they were building to the tune of $220 million—the largest construction project in the state that year—was done for.

Newt told John Berger exactly what went wrong:

"They killed the goose that laid the golden egg," Becker said. "I blame the [state] Finance Department, because if

*Newt speaking at the
official opening of the
first Luz plant.
Arnold Goldman is seated,
third from the left (1985)*

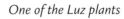

One of the Luz plants

*Rows of Luz parabolic
troughs that follow the
sun (1985)*

they had brought out their concerns early, we could have addressed their concerns during the committee hearings within both houses. By sneaking this in at the last second, they killed the solar [thermal electric power] industry...If they'd been upfront, we could have addressed their concerns, but they stabbed us in the back instead, through the governor."

As Alexis Madrigal, author of *Powering the Dream: The History and Promise of Green Technology*, points out, despite Luz's demise, Newt was always thinking about the future, and though the company was in Chapter 7 in 1991, he wanted those tax cuts to be made permanent, even if they would come too late to benefit Luz directly. He wrote an article for *Solar Today* magazine, *The Demise of Luz: A Case Study*, and testified before the House Ways and Means Committee on February 10, 1992. As Madrigal states:

After the company's untimely demise, Newton Becker went before Congress to deliver a fiery oration about the irrationality of American energy policy. "As an investor I am here much like the crime victim trying to change a law," he said. His testimony, which quickly summarized the whole lot of unfairness and regulatory silliness, demonstrated the tremendous carelessness of U.S. energy policy. He noted that the time to plan for the energy supply of the future is when those resources are adequate and cheap. That also happens to be the time when Americans are most likely to ignore the problem. "Without greater attention by Government, we are doomed to breathing foul air and increasingly relying on unstable countries in the Middle East as a major source of our country's energy."

NEWTON D. BECKER, PH.D., CPA

The Demise of Luz: A Case Study

The world's largest producer of solar-thermal electricity files for bankruptcy as a result of policy and regulatory obstacles.

On November 25, 1991, Luz International Ltd. and four subsidiaries filed for bankruptcy. Luz International and subsidiaries Luz Development and Finance Corporation and Luz Construction Inc. filed for liquidation of the company's assets under Chapter 7, while Luz Partnership Management Inc. and Luz Engineering Corporation filed under Chapter 11, which permits reorganization of the businesses to assure continued operation of the nine existing plants. These filings signal the likely end of the large-scale solar-thermal electric industry for the foreseeable future. The sequence of events that led to the demise of Luz is testimony to this country's lack of a coherent energy policy.

A Brief History

Since Luz was founded in early 1980, it has successfully developed, constructed and arranged the financing for nine solar thermal electric energy plants. The plants are located in the Mojave Desert and supply Southern California with 354 megawatts (MW) of installed capacity. This is enough energy to supply the residential needs of 540,000 people during peak periods of use.

The first two plants (14 MW and 30 MW) were built in 1984 and 1985 and produced electricity at a cost of 24 cents per kilowatt hour (kWh). The next five were 30 MW plants built in the years 1986 to 1988. They produced electricity at 12 cents per kWh. The two 80 MW plants built in 1989

and 1990 produced electricity at 8 cents per kWh. The next generation of Luz solar plants to be constructed in 1994-95 were projected to produce electricity at a cost of approximately 6 to 6 1/2 cents per kWh. In comparison, new nuclear plants today are "projected" to produce electricity at 6 cents to 9 cents a kWh—with no cost overruns. Natural gas electrical generation is now at 6 to 7 cents per kWh and coal (depending on pollution controls) is at about 4 to 6 cents.

The steady reductions in cost for solar thermal electricity are largely a result of corrective feedback from the operation of the earlier plants. Reductions in component costs, improved efficiency in the collector systems and economies of scale derived from larger plants all contributed to lower costs.

Since the solar thermal electric generating industry is still an infant industry, these projected improvements in cost, efficiency and scale will not end with the next generation. Improved maintenance regimes and more research and development will continue to reduce costs.

Some financial models have indicated that a natural gas turbine combined with a solar field could produce electricity in the 4 to 5 cent range. This could be accomplished by using a higher percentage of natural gas to solar than the 25 percent currently allowable under PURPA (see sidebar, page 26) rules governing independent power producers.

Beginning of the End

Since 1987, the federal solar energy tax credit has been subject to renewal on an annual basis. As a result of this policy, Luz launched an expensive and time consuming lobbying effort every year to ensure the renewal of the federal solar energy tax credit. In December, 1989, Congress fully renewed all credits in an extender bill that expired September 30, 1990.

Since the economic viability of a Solar Electric Generating System (SEGS) is dependent on the availability of federal and state energy tax credits to its investors, the September 30th expiration date for the credits forced Luz to build its ninth solar plant (SEGS IX) in a period of about seven and a half months. The rush to complete the plant meant that highly paid union employees worked a great deal of overtime and that Luz was compelled to hire subcontractors without enough time to ensure competitive bidding. The total field construction budget increased by about 50 percent, a total cost overrun of over $30 million.

This cost overrun was not absorbed by investors in the plant, but by the Luz shareholders. Three-quarters of the company's $45 million retained earnings was wiped out in that one "rush" project. Nevertheless, the company continued its operations in the hope of making up for the loss in the subsequent three projects for which it had power purchase contracts with Southern California Edison, SEGS X, XI and XII.

Newt's article in the January/February 1992 issue of Solar Today magazine

In playing Monday-morning Luz quarterback, there are other things that can be deduced that hurt the enterprise. For one, the price of oil, after the scare of the 1970s, had become very cheap by the mid-1980s. Without the high price of fossil fuels, it became difficult to ratchet up the political pressure for the government to do the things it needed to allow for renewables to compete effectively in the energy marketplace.

There was something else at work here, as Scott Sklar pointed out. The best thing that ever happened to the solar industry was Jimmy Carter. The worst thing that ever happened to the industry was Ronald Reagan. While he may have revitalized the American spirit and done in the Soviet Union, Reagan liked those solar panels on the White House about as much as he liked the Berlin Wall. He might have urged Mr. Gorbachev to tear down the latter, but he took it upon himself to do away with the former. It might have been a symbolic action, but it spoke volumes about how he felt about solar and renewable energy.

The great irony is that in the election of 1980, many Israel advocates campaigned for the defeat of Carter after his relationship with the Jewish community deteriorated during the course of his administration. In 1976, he had received 71 percent of the Jewish vote. By 1980, he received only 45 percent of the Jewish vote, the lowest total for any Democrat since James Cox lost in 1920 to Warren G. Harding. Though the Jewish community would tangle with the new administration over some issues, Reagan was considered across the entire political spectrum to be a great friend of the Jews and Israel, and shared many of Newt's feelings about the need to spread freedom and democracy throughout the world. But in this sphere of solar and renewables, the Reagan administration and his vice president who succeeded him (George H. W. Bush), were not good. Luz and Newt paid a heavy price for it. It is interesting to note, however, that although the administration was unfriendly to it, for the most part Luz succeeded during the period until the very end. Perhaps this in itself is another great Newt Becker lesson in how to maneuver your way around obstacles.

Newt had lost his investment in Luz, but if one expected him to remain bitter and call it a day in the field of renewables, one would have been sadly mistaken. The technology of Luz, developed in Israel, reverted to the Israeli government, who had helped underwrite the research and development plan. It was then purchased by a European outfit. Arnold Goldman founded another company, this one named Electric Fuel, which developed and produced an innovative battery for electric cars, trucks and buses. Newt served as the founding chairman until January 1993, when he was replaced by Robert Ehrlich. The company had some Luz people, but it became apparent as the company went public, that it was not interested in listening to its largest shareholder. Newt began to disapprove of the direction that the company was taking and decided to sell his holdings. Given how extensive they were, this was a gradual process, but with the high-tech boom market of the mid- and late 1990s, Electric Fuel turned out to be a winner, or so the stock market thought. Newt did well from Electric Fuel, and as no one will be surprised to hear, nearly all of the money he made from the investment went to the Foundation. It was almost as if powers up above were rewarding him for all of the blood, sweat, and tears that he had put into Luz. Remarkably, Luz' plants that were built in the 1980s are still operating well today.

GM's EV1

NEWT AND HIS EV 1

Electric vehicles, like solar energy, are not new concepts at all. Electric cars go back to the early days of the automobile, but like other renewables, were done in by the internal combustion engine. Many believed that resistance to the concept, and the lack of research and development necessary to make it work, were because the major companies were so invested in their old ways. Just as they had been slow to react to competition for more fuel-efficient cars that came from Japan during the 1970s, they were slow to react to the mounting environmental concerns in the '90s.

Despite all of this, GM demonstrated the Impact, an electric concept car at the Los Angeles Auto Show in 1990. By 1996, GM came to market with its first electric car, the EV1 (Electric Vehicle 1). It was a two-door and two-seat coupe and it was offered only as a lease. There were plenty of skeptics and the price was not cheap. Only 288 people signed up for a lease that first year. The most famous was the actor Tom Hanks, who talked it up in the media. There was someone with a lower profile who also leased an EV1 that first year. Yep, Newton D. Becker. The man who loved convertibles loved breakthrough technology and weaning the world off of oil even more. He became a huge fan of the car. He relished the opportunity to take visitors for rides in it and no fewer than a dozen people whom I spoke to remembered such an excursion. It was a novelty for many people and occasionally provided for some humor. Once, Newt took his young grandson, Brandon, for a ride. Many years later, and now a college student, Brandon still recalls it vividly:

He took me to the Petersen Auto Museum on Wilshire Boulevard, and then we just kept driving around, and he's taking me to see all of these cool things and we are having a great time. All of sudden something happens and I don't even know what it is, but we are out of electricity and right in the middle of the street. We get out of the car and he pushes it all the way to Gelson's (a large grocery store) parking lot because they had a charger there. So he plugs it in, and I thought it was like going to the gas station and we would leave in ten minutes. But it took four hours, a really slow process to get the electricity going. He wasn't really too happy and just sat reading magazines until we had enough of a charge to go on. By now it was nighttime, and on the freeway there was heavy traffic. The car in front of us stopped short and the car in back of us rear-ended us. It wasn't a bad accident but the bumper *came off, and after exchanging information with the other drivers, he put the bumper on my lap. Finally after the two-hour ride, we arrived home long after my bedtime. He was worried about what my parents might say, so he offered me a $100 bill if I said nothing. For $100, my lips were sealed. Of course, my parents wondered how the bumper came off, and so he said, "Oh that, it's nothing. It just kinda came off."*

It may have been Newt's only bribe.

General Motors made the fateful decision in 2003 to cancel the second generation of the EV1. As was reported, "At least 58 EV1 drivers sent letters and deposit checks to GM, requesting lease extensions at no risk or cost to the automaker. The drivers agreed to be responsible for the maintenance and repair costs of the EV1, and would allow GM the right to terminate the lease if expensive repairs were needed. On June 28, GM famously refused the offer and returned the checks, which totaled $22,000." In sympathy with them, Newt was furious with the company. It appeared it never had its heart in electric vehicles, nor in a lot else, and by the end of the decade it had plunged into bankruptcy.

Newt would not beg off electric cars and switched to a Toyota RAV4 EV, one of only a few fully electric cars available. Whereas the EV1 that he leased was a red sports car that was exciting and stylish, the RAV4 was a barebones small SUV and many who would happily drive an EV1 eschewed the RAV4 EV.

Rochelle Becker remembers going to meetings with Newt's lawyers at Hillcrest Country Club. While waiting for

*A RAV4 similar
to the one
Newt owned.*

their lawyers—and these were high-priced folks—to enter their Bentleys, Jaguars, or Mercedes, Newt would get into his RAV4 EV. Rochelle noted the irony. No matter how many times wealthier than the other person Newt may have been, he paid no mind to appearances. He was just so comfortable in his own skin, even if a touch cramped in his electric car.

IBEP

You are running a big operation with locations all over the country; you're preparing students for the CPA exam; you are chairman of a cutting-edge solar energy company; plus you are heavily involved in a wide variety of philanthropic activities. For most people, it sounds like a pretty busy schedule and a pretty full plate. Not for Newt Becker.

As in so many areas, Newt was ahead of his time when it came to investing. In the last couple of years, there has been a spate of books detailing Israel's economic rise, particularly in technology and science. It is only very recently that anyone ever thought it a desirable locale for investors. Given its founding as a socialist country, its powerful labor unions, its complicated political structure and heavy government bureaucracy, high taxes, costly wars, heavy defense spending, absorption of large numbers of immigrants in nearly every decade of its existence, limited natural resources, and small land mass, and given that it is being threatened with extinction by some of its neighbors, one would imagine that Israel would be the last place to invest one's money. This author remembers a prominent American professor in the late 1970s making the case that the hot Mediterranean climate was too much of an impediment to the running of a successful economy. There was always that joke, "How do you make a small fortune in Israel? Go there with a large one."

Newt Becker did not see it that way. As Steve Rosen mentioned, Newt thought the major impediment was the political situation. Once that changed, the economy had great potential. The situation changed ever so slowly in 1977, with the two-decade break in the power of the Labor Party. Menachem Begin was much more open to a freer economy; he cut subsidies to the kibbutzim and promised to bring privatization to a country with many nationalized industries.

Of course, many Jews in Western countries invested in Israel because they wanted to help the country. While Newt spent his whole life in the service of his people and the State of Israel, he looked at investing in Israel also as an opportunity with great potential.

Israel Rosen was a dealmaker out of New York with extensive contacts in Israel. He had, starting in the late '70s, put

*Rochelle and
Newt (1999)*

together a series of limited partnerships that focused on technology including bioengineering and the pharmaceutical industry. His investors were primarily American and Canadian Jews, and all together he created eleven investment partnerships. The one that we are concerned with is Israel Bio-Engineering Project, known as IBEP. In 1982, IBEP sold 113 units of the partnership, and the following year it sold 48 units, for a total of over $9,500,000. The Israeli government, through its Office of the Chief Scientist, in a policy designed to encourage investment in research, participated in this funding effort by granting a loan to the limited partners.

It was all a very complicated arrangement. Research would be done at the renowned Weizmann Institute of Science in Rehovot. Yeda, the arm of the Weizmann Institute responsible for commercializing the research, had created a company called Inter-Yeda, a joint venture between Yeda and Inter-pharm, which was an Israeli subsidiary of the large Swiss pharmaceutical company, known as Serono. Serono, having been acquired by Merck, is now known as Merck Serono.

The following summary of the arrangement made, from one of the many synopses that can be found in the public record, should make this a little clearer:

> IBEP signed three research agreements with Inter-Yeda in December 1982 which were set to expire in December 1987. Under the agreements, IBEP would fund a number of research programs and in return IBEP would have all ownership rights, title, and interest in patents and pat-ent applications resulting from the agreements. At the same time, Inter-Yeda received an option to purchase the research results in return for certain royalties and license fees payable to the partnership.

In a bit of an unusual development that would significantly impact our story, while trying to get his 161 units sold, Rosen found himself unable to sell the final 10 units. He, therefore, sold the 10 units to Serono, which for a pharmaceutical com-pany, proved to be highly unusual in such a limited partnership.

Whether in Israel or anywhere in the world, such an investment is highly risky. One is betting that research can eventually be turned into something that will have a commer-cial application. Though Newt was the largest investor, he was still a limited partner, so, for the duration of the partnership all he could do was hope and read the partnership updates that Israel Rosen would provide.

In 1990, Israel Rosen passed away. As the general partner, he ran the day-to-day business of the partnership. Fortunately, in the other partnerships that Rosen put together, when it was time to discern the status of the partnerships, Bernard Sterling, a CPA, had become a liquidating trustee for most of them. When it came to IBEP, Sterling determined for the partners that based on what he knew, there was value, certainly enough to warrant further investigation, and he offered to serve as liquidating trustee.

Gerald Cohen and Richard Levine, two of the limited partners, had other ideas. They thought that the unusual opportunity of having Newt as the largest investor should be realized by having him appointed liquidating trustee. He was an "accountant's accountant," as so many have described him, and with his excellent contacts in Israel, could navigate the terrain as well as anyone. At first Newt politely declined, perhaps feeling his plate was full enough. Finally, he relented, and starting in 1992, by vote of the majority of the partners, he took over as liquidating trustee.

For all of Newt's challenges—building Becker CPA and Luz from the ground up, building MEMRI with Yigal Carmon from much the same—his tenure as liquidating trustee at IBEP would prove to be perhaps his most challenging assignment. Ascertaining the value and the status of the research required scientific and legal talent, and Newt traveled to Israel to assemble a team of top-flight people.

While Newt's strategy was sound, there was only one problem. The partnership had no money and the anticipated legal fees would be considerable, especially considering that they would be mixing it up with large pharmaceutical companies who often employed their considerable financial resources to full advantage. Newt proposed to the partnership that it should borrow money to fund the legal costs. All of the limited partners were invited to participate in the loan program although Newt informed them all that he would take up any slack should some partners prefer not to participate. Though some others put money in, it was Newt who bore about 80 percent of the loan. It was very risky, a non-recourse loan at 18 percent; and unless the legal action produced something, it would not be repaid, which would mean a total loss for the lender.

So now Newt stood to lose even more than his initial investment. But he had more than a gut feeling that it could be worthwhile and so he essentially doubled down on money and commitment. Serono's attempt to dissolve the partnership was a good sign. Later, it would tender a lowball offer to settle. That was another good sign. The legal case, such as it was, took place on two continents. The Israeli case began in 1993, and is still going strong twenty years later. Since the case is still in litigation, the discussion here is limited, with the focus on what the IBEP experience teaches us about Newt.

The Talmud tells us that everything requires mazel, even a Torah scroll in the Ark. And of the eleven Israel Rosen limited partnerships, IBEP had the most mazel. From those five years of funded research, there emerged key elements leading to the development of five blockbuster drugs. Humira, Enbrel, and Remicade are three essentially identical drugs that treat arthritis and Crohn's disease. In 2011, they were the 10th, 11th and 12th biggest selling drugs on the market with combined annual sales of more than $10 billion. Avonex and Rebif are essentially identical to each other and are used for treating multiple sclerosis. They were ranked the 33rd and 52nd biggest selling drugs with combined sales of $2.5 billion. The IBEP partners believe that they are owed *substantial* royalties and license fees that Serono has refused to pay.

Drug companies are known for being difficult and litigious but there was one thing that the behemoth drug companies which have been involved in the litigation did not count on: Newton D. Becker.

Newt's lawyer, Orrin Persky, and his scientific expert, Raymond Kaempfer, have commented on how impressed they were by Newt's handling of the case. For nineteen years, as with everything else he did, he was completely hands-on. As with solar energy, he showed his capacity to understand scientific information that very few laymen and not all professionals could have handled. In addition to his ability to grasp complex amounts of information, these legal and scientific experts who served on the IBEP team admired his creativity, toughness, patience, endurance, and determination. Orrin Persky pointed out that he was most impressed with Newt's continued capacity to analyze situations deeply and effectively without letting his emotions get in the way. For most people in such charged circumstances, their emotions play something of a role. Not Newt.

In many respects, though he may not have wished for what the IBEP project would become, the struggle was tailor-made for Newt. In the face-off against the drug companies, it was a classic David versus Goliath, the kind of odds that Newt specialized in. And in the end, the result could have substituted as a narrative for Newt's life, success, and ongoing struggle.

*Rochelle and Newt at
Rochelle's Surprise
Birthday party (2000)*

*David, Newt and
Dan (2002)*

While several of the drug companies have made some royalty payments, such payments have been accompanied by a seemingly never ending legal battle, or, better said, legal battles. Newt never showed signs of letting up or slowing down. His determination was absolute. While ill in 2011, seven months before he passed away, Newt traveled to Israel for such a battle, one in which he would testify in court. It involved eight days of preparation and two days of testifying. Despite health challenges, he refused to relent.

When Newt agreed to become liquidating trustee in 1992 he could never have imagined that this battle would continue for so long. In his last piece of correspondence to his fellow partners, Newt told it like it was, and predicted that the legal wrangles could last another nine years. That was a worst-case scenario, but no matter how long, Newt was prepared to continue. In the event that he could not outlive his adversaries, and, sadly, this turned out to be the case, he appointed his son, David, and his son-in-law, Andy, talented men both, to carry on. As of this writing, the lawsuits continue and the size of the potential judgment is huge. The vast majority of the Becker share will go to Newt's charitable foundations.

We have spoken about some of his most consequential investments. In most of his investments, he did not play as active a role as he did with Luz, Electric Fuel, or IBEP. Whether it was circumstances that propelled him into his role, or just his desire, he enjoyed investing far beyond its financial angle. He was always looking for where the future was headed and hoped to be there before anyone else.

There were many investment professionals who worked with Newt on his portfolio. Newt's way was to be trusting until proven otherwise. Given his schedule, he just didn't have the time to micromanage and had to trust others. Just as with the incident of finding that someone had defrauded him while working in his employ, it was discovered that one of his professional advisers had indeed absconded with funds.

This was at a large national brokerage firm, and the man was stealing money from customer accounts to cover bad trades that he was making. He had circumvented nearly every internal control that the firm was supposed to be enforcing. The amount stolen out of Newt's account was in the small seven figures. The firm was hesitating to make Newt whole even though it was clearly its responsibility. Frustrated over its dilly-dallying, Newt composed a formidable letter to the company, pointing out its egregious errors and lack of taking responsibility would make for a great story in the local paper.

The firm finally realized that this Newt Becker was an unusual man. In breeching its fiduciary responsibilities, it had opened itself up for significant litigation, something it was at pains to avoid, and changed its tone considerably. Newt came back with his terms. He wanted his money back with interest. The penalties due him, however, which would have amounted to $500,000 or so, he did not want. Instead, the brokerage firm would take that money and contribute it to Bet Tzedek, an organization based in Los Angeles that provides free legal services to those who cannot afford them.

Tzedek is a Hebrew word that means righteousness. The Bible states, *Tzedek, Tzedek Tirdof,* which translates to "Righteousness, righteousness you shall pursue." The Biblical commentators ask the question of why the word *Tzedek* is repeated. One of the answers given is not only must you live and act righteously and justly, but the manner in which you pursue righteousness must itself be righteous. That was Newt Becker. He sought to use an opportunity in which he was wronged, not as the means to improve his own situation or to punish people, but to do good. Revenge may be a dish best served cold, but it was never on Newt's menu.

The money was to fund a law library, something the organization's staff desperately needed. Newt was a man, who as we have seen throughout his upbringing and later life, felt to be the exemplification of the underdog. That was simply how he saw himself. What made him unique was that he continued to see himself that way long after his success was clearly established. Perhaps most importantly, he realized that his good fortune meant that he owed something to those less fortunate. If he pursued a legal case, as he did with the ADA case at Becker, it was because he realized that those less powerful than he could not have pursued it. He was, in effect, representing them. When it came to the theft at the brokerage firm, the same was true. Investors who had lost a modest sum probably did not have the clout to assert their rights the way Newt did.

There was a lesson in what it takes to make a big and profitable organization do the right thing. It frequently has to be forced into it. It was only when the firm realized that the negative publicity could cost it not just millions but tens of millions that it finally agreed to Newt's terms.

As for the broker who stole millions, he was disgraced and apparently could stand it no more. He took his own life. So ended this sad chapter.

CHAPTER SEVEN

Israel
Advocate

Newt was known for taking out-of-town guests, friends, relatives, and even some grantees to some of his favorite Southern California spots. There were beaches, boardwalks, and museums. One of his favorite places was the Hollywood Bowl. The Bowl was only six years older than Newt and has long maintained an iconic status in a city not lacking in icons.

Newt made his first visit to the Bowl about two years after relocating to Los Angeles. The date was June 11, 1967, and he was part of an overflow crowd of more than eighteen thousand people. Frank Sinatra and Barbara Streisand were there, but not to give a concert. The overflow crowd was there for serious business—a rally jointly sponsored by the Jewish Federation of Los Angeles and Israel Bonds. Its principal purpose was to marshal support for the state of Israel and to raise much-needed funds. The main speaker that June day was the governor of California, Ronald Wilson Reagan. Though he had been warned to avoid such a partisan event, Governor Reagan delivered a riveting defense of the Jewish state. His

165

appearance is said to have paid dividends when he ran for president.

Why was there a need for such a gathering of celebrities and regular supporters of Israel alike? June 11 was a Sunday, and the previous Monday, June 5, marked the beginning of what would be known as the Six Day War—a conflict that would change the map of the Jewish state and the state of the Jewish spirit. It is essential to understanding Newt because the events of the war and its aftermath paved the way for Israel advocacy.

Since the war was critical to what would be the activities of Newt Becker it is worth reviewing its history. Newt is often associated with the organization named MEMRI, the Middle East Media Research Institute, charged with translating selected articles and television segments from the Arab and Muslim media into English. Had MEMRI been around at the onset of the war it would have been translating the following from Egypt: "The armies of Egypt, Jordan, Syria and Lebanon are stationed on the borders of Israel. Behind them stand the armies of Iraq, Algeria, Kuwait, Sudan, and the whole of the Arab nation. . . . We intend to open a general assault. This will be total war. Our basic aim is the destruction of Israel." From Syria: "Our forces are now entirely ready not only to repulse any aggression, but to initiate the act ourselves, and to explode the Zionist presence in the Arab homeland of Palestine. The Syrian army, with its finger on the trigger, is united. I believe that the time has come to begin a battle of annihilation." And from Iraq: "The existence of Israel is an error which must be rectified. This is our opportunity to wipe out the ignominy which has been with us since 1948. Our goal is clear—to wipe Israel off the map."

With this kind of language and with Arab armies ready to pounce on many fronts, and after Egypt blocked the Straits of Tiran which was a legal act of war, Israel felt it could wait no longer and decided to strike first. On Monday, June 5, Israel attacked the Egyptian air force, destroying its airfields and its planes that were on the ground. While its own country was completely open to attack, through a combination of daring and the Divine, the air war and the ground war that followed, were resounding successes. Despite being outmanned and outgunned, Israel managed to defeat Egypt, Iraq, Jordan, and Syria within six days. Israel gained the Sinai Desert and the Golan Heights, unified Jerusalem and brought the West Bank under Jewish control for the first time since the Roman invasion.

As a result of the war, the attitudes of many American Jews went through a metamorphosis. Whereas there had always been a core of committed Zionists, there was a minority of Jews who were either non-Zionists or anti-Zionists. The Holocaust convinced many of the importance of a Jewish state, and the Six Day War led most of the rest of the organized Jewish community to support Zionism. As an example, the American Jewish Committee, which had always represented itself as "non-Zionist," suddenly got on the Israel bandwagon. *Commentary Magazine*, which was sponsored by the American Jewish Committee at the time, would eventually become a leading voice in support of the Jewish state.

The anti-Zionist American Council for Judaism, an influential organization, particularly among Reform Jews, became marginalized after the war. There is the story of a chapter president of the organization who was so inspired by the Israeli victory that he traveled to Israel and, by 1968, was chairman of the Israel Bond Drive in his city.

It should be mentioned that there was another group of Jews who was completely transformed by the war. The Jews of Russia—who had endured the czars, a dreadful civil war, a communist revolution, an invasion by the Nazi horde, and Joseph Stalin—were reawakened. They were awash with pride over the Israeli victory. A group of activists known as Refuseniks developed who had pride in their Jewish past and who planned on emigrating to Israel. With the collapse of the Soviet Union, Jews would leave en-masse. In the 1990s, nearly a million of them would go to Israel. They would play a substantial role in the great high-tech economy that we spoke about in the last chapter.

It was not just Jews, whether Israeli, American, or Russian, who were affected by the war. Many non-Jews were filled with admiration for the sheer audacity of the tiny country. The myth of the Jew as powerless victim was completely shattered in 1967. It was as if Jewish history, and particularly the Nazi rise in the 1930s, had now been stood on its head. To get a sense of just how dramatic the change had been it is worth taking a quick detour to the state of Jewish life in 1930s. Our guide is Bernard Wasserstein, a distinguished historian who has recently written a highly acclaimed book that chronicles Jewish life shortly before the Second World War. The first paragraph of *On the Eve*, reads this way:

> *A specter haunted Europe in the 1930s—the specter of the Jew. Simultaneously feared and despised as a Christ-killer, a devil with horns, subversive revolutionary and capitalist exploiter, obdurate upholder of an outmoded religion and devious exponent of cultural modernism, the Jew was widely regarded as an alien presence. Increasingly*

excluded from normal society and extruded from common human fellowship, the Jew was transmogrified from fellow into bogey, a subhuman, at best an inconvenience, eventually almost everywhere a hunted beast. Even before the outbreak of the Second World War, this was true not just in those areas of Europe already directly ruled by the Nazis but over the greater part of the continent.

The Israeli, and the Jew by extension, was now transformed once more, but this time it was in a heroic way. America, whose very creation rested on the defeat of a vast empire, has always identified with an underdog and largely fell in love with the Israeli model. While the victory was an Israeli one and a Jewish one, the way in which it was accomplished simply resonated with Americans.

There was another stunning historical reversal. With the unification of Jerusalem, and Jewish control of areas like Bethlehem, Jewish soldiers would be protecting modern-day Christian pilgrims, and one of the first things that the Israeli authorities did after the war was make explicit their intention to allow all religions free access to their holy sites. Contrast this with the Medieval Crusades, where Christian soldiers, under the pretense of making the Holy Land safe for Christian pilgrims, massacred Jews, both on the way to the Middle East and in Israel, while fighting the Muslims. Now, it would be the Jews who would be protecting Christians and Muslims alike. Naturally, for some Christians, 1948 and later 1967 led to greater eschatological fervor, but for most, they identified with Israel just as so many other Americans did, for moral reasons, as well as for military and strategic ones. They would eventually become valuable allies in the political movement we call

"Israel advocacy." Christian Zionists, as some Evangelicals would be called, became passionate supporters of the state. It was support that Newt Becker welcomed and encouraged.

Getting back to the war itself, it is important to bear in mind that the euphoria that Jews like Newt Becker felt about the dramatic Israeli victory was genuinely tempered by a deep sense of relief and the gnawing feeling that it all could have gone very differently. Three *Newsweek* journalists who had covered the war, Edward Klein, Richard Chesnoff, and Robert Littell, were thinking along those lines and were struck by two statements—one from Golda Meir and the other from Yitzhak Rabin—that seemed to confirm those feelings. From Golda came: "Just imagine if Nasser had gotten to our airfields first. What would have happened if he had bombed out our airfields while the planes were on the ground, or if he had bombed them while our planes were in the air? That was our constant nightmare before the war." Rabin stated: "A successful first air strike by the Arabs would have been decisive. Some people say, 'Oh, yes, but what about the Americans?' I would hate to be in a position where the existence of Israel depended on the United States." His statement points not only to how vulnerable the state was while carrying out the strike but just how tenuous was the relationship between the United States and Israel until after the war. Rabin was not just trying to score a political point or exerting his usual bravado when he said, "I would hate to be in a position where the existence of Israel depended on the United States." At the time, it could not be counted on. And it was only after the Six Day War that the notion of a special relationship between the two countries developed, one that advocates like Newt Becker helped foster.

The three *Newsweek* writers whom we spoke of above decided to write a novel about what would have happened had the Egyptians struck first in June of 1967. It is not a pretty piece of alternate history but a stark and scary one titled simply, *If Israel Lost the War: A Novel.* What are most frightening are not the actual pieces of fiction, for they are mere fiction: ninety-three thousand IDF soldiers killed; one hundred thousand Israeli civilians killed. Moshe Dayan publicly executed. The world community turning its collective back on the Jews for the second time (the first being the Holocaust) and no help from President Johnson. A bloody occupation follows, complete with pogroms, mass rapes, and a policy of forced migrations.

What was most frightening about the book was not so much the detail but the gnawing knowledge that it all could have happened that way. Most disturbing in the book perhaps was the failure of the United States to act in Israel's defense. This was the type of scenario that had haunted Newton Becker. This was his worst fear, and he took it upon himself to make sure that *If Israel Lost the War,* or anything like it, would always be read as fiction and never as fact.

Central to such a task would be the building of the relationship so that America would not see itself as neutral in the conflict, or as so many urged it to be, simply an honest broker between two parties. Newt wanted America to see itself as a friend that would act on the other's behalf. That the United States would do just that six years later, with the savage attack of the Yom Kippur War, is a testament to the work of Israel advocates like Newton Becker. One of the organizations that was developed to strengthen that relationship was the American Israel Public Affairs Committee, known as AIPAC.

When I met Newt at AIPAC's Annual Conference in 2011, it was an intimate gathering of around eleven thousand souls. Nearly anybody who was of importance in our nation's capitol made an appearance. No one dared skip this event and politicians could be observed holding court. Some held private receptions. They all seemed to be outdoing one another in espousing their pro-Israel bonafides. It was not the United States as neutral or honest broker, but the United States and Israel together as friends and partners.

How did AIPAC do it, and how did Israel advocacy travel so long a distance in so short a period of time? How did it go from 1948, when the American government enforced a strict boycott on weapons that would have helped the Jews of Palestine and actively prosecuted American citizens who helped get weapons in, to 1956, when the United States actively opposed Israel in the Suez Campaign to the neutrality of 1967, to the emergency sending of arms and equipment in 1973, which many believe saved Israel?

Steve Rosen, one of the most important and effective officials at AIPAC, who contributed mightily to its phenomenal growth, enjoyed a long friendship with Newt Becker. The two met in the 1970s when Steve was a professor of political science and was a major voice on campus for Israel advocacy. Steve thrived so much in this role which included giving testimony to the Senate Foreign Relations Committee about Saudi arms sales that after a time at the Rand Corporation where he saw a lot of Newt, he decided to make Israel advocacy a full-time career. Steve joined AIPAC in 1982, and eventually became a top official there. In addition to sharing a broader friendship, they spoke frequently on matters relating to politics, Israel, and the Middle East.

Steve still remembers a conversation, circa mid-80s that the two had about the AIPAC budget. It perhaps reveals better than any other story in this book the sense of responsibility that Newt felt. It is hard to imagine any other American Jewish leader, and this is with great respect to the commitment of Newt's fellow philanthropists, expressing these sentiments. When it came to such matters, Newt was just plain different:

"Newt and I were speaking about the enormous growth of AIPAC. He then asked me what AIPAC's budget was, and I informed him that it had risen to four and a half million dollars. He looked a bit perplexed and then said, "Oh, gee, it's four and a half million, is it? You know something Steve? I've always thought to myself that if all the other Jews got scared and backed away, I could pay the whole AIPAC budget myself. And I gladly would have. But this is the first year it got too big for me to handle. If they all run away, I won't be able to cover the budget. This is the first year I won't be able to do it." And this was something he worried about all the time. It occupied his thoughts over and over again. He had taken all of this on himself and felt very down because at that moment he realized that he could not be the personal guarantor of the State of Israel. He could not handle the burden alone, and it was a very upsetting thought for him."

In this story, we also can note the demarcation between the Newton Becker approach to leadership and advocacy and the type that he associated with a previous generation, with people like Rabbi Stephen Wise. Rabbi Wise, had the strongest relationship with FDR of all Jewish leaders, but when it

came time for him to press the man he lionized, he simply
cowered. Newt detested such a mentality. The fear in the back
of his mind was that pressure, and charges of dual loyalty
would make Jewish leaders lose their nerve.

As devoted as Newt was to AIPAC, and he was very
devoted indeed, he did not walk in lockstep with it. I am not
speaking here about policy issues but rather about what is
acknowledged by many as the organization's most difficult
hour. For whatever reason, and it is beyond our scope, AIPAC
did not always stand by its people. One of the two people
it did not stand with was Steve Rosen, who together with a
colleague, was indicted by the U.S. Justice Department with
charges relating to the espionage case of Lawrence Franklin.

The ordeal began in 2005. Six months after it began, AIPAC
decided to extricate itself from the whole business and fired
Steve. So there he was, left out in the cold, facing a legal battle
against the U.S. government, the one entity that Newt Becker
knew as well as anyone possessed unlimited resources. Steve
Rosen reached out to his friend Newt, and before offering his
help Newt only wanted to know one thing: Would Steve cut a
deal with the government? While this is always a temptation
when faced with the alternative, Steve, as an innocent man,
refused to even consider it. That was all Newt wanted to hear,
and he promised to support him all the way—which he did.

When Newt got behind an idea, as we have seen, he went
all out. When he got behind a person, he went even further.
The manner of assistance he lent was material, spiritual, and
moral. As Steve relates what that support meant to him and
his family, he minced no words: "Newt Becker saved my
life." The FBI thought it could dissuade Newt from standing
by his friend, but they should have known that the man from

Glenville just could not be intimidated. After two visits, Newt let them know they would be well served not to make a third. They took his advice. The government eventually backed away from Steve as well, and in 2009 dropped all charges. But it was four years of hell, and Newt Becker, who knew something of what it was like to be on the wrong side of the U.S. government from his own ordeal at Becker CPA, helped stay the course.

Newt was also endowed with boundless energy. Despite the seriousness of the topics he dealt with, he displayed the type of energy—physical, intellectual, and emotional—that one finds in someone decades younger. Yigal Carmon describes an experience with his indefatigable friend this way.

I shall never forget the day I took Newt for a tour of Israel's border. Starting out from Jerusalem at six-thirty in the morning, we proceeded through Jericho and the Jordan Valley, where we visited different sites along the border; then the Golan Heights—which we crisscrossed east and west—to Mount Hermon, up and down and along the Lebanese border, visiting various places. We finally arrived at Kibbutz Rosh HaNikra at around eight-thirty in the evening, much later than I expected. Rosh HaNikra, which is now privatized, has a state-of-the-art laboratory that does in-vitro plant propagation, and knowing Newt's interest in biotechnology and Israeli biotechnology, I had arranged for us to tour the plant. But by now I was completely exhausted and was hoping Newt was the same so we could skip the tour. Instead, he said, "Where is the plant? and, "C'mon let's go." To try and get a little rest before we drove to Jerusalem, I told Newt that I had some phone calls to make and dropped to sleep in the car.

He emerged about an hour and a half later, after having inspected every inch of the laboratory floor. On the way to Jerusalem, he could not stop analyzing in great detail all that he had seen.

The fearlessness in Newt that we referred to earlier could be a double-edged sword. It was the fiery and dauntless Frederick Douglass who was quoted as saying, "One and God make a majority." That was pretty much how Newt went about talking to people, whether it was about Israel advocacy or, as we shall see in the next chapter, democracy defense organizations. Like Frederick Douglass, he believed unshakably in the cause he was espousing but he knew that more supporters were needed. He had such a conviction about what he believed that, particularly when dealing with other wealthy people, he sometimes spoke to them in a way they were not used to. There were times when such a lack of diplomacy was warranted; there were other times when it put him at odds with some fellow philanthropists. But Newt Becker was not out to endear himself to anyone. He was out to change the world.

Of course, it was not all toil and trouble. There were certain benefits for those in leadership positions. Rochelle Becker remembers an event held at the home of their friends, the Weinbergs, who were also major Israel advocates. Larry Weinberg was not only a prominent real estate developer at the time but an owner of the Portland Trail Blazers basketball team. Upon entering their home, Rochelle Becker ended up sitting with an old lady, hair in a bun, and sporting orthopedic shoes. She was, of course, Golda Meir, the prime minister of the State of Israel, a lady who, like Rochelle, had come of age in the Midwest.

Rochelle and Newt with Prime Minister Golda Meir (~1973)

Prime Minister Menachem Begin, Rochelle and Newt (~1977)

Newt (top of ladder) arriving in Israel on a
Jewish Federation "Mission" (~1979)

Newt and others from the mission at the Western Wall;
Irwin Field is third from left (~1979)

A few minutes later, Newt and Rochelle were formally introduced to Prime Minister Meir just before getting their picture taken with her. Newt, aware that Golda started her career as a schoolteacher and referring to his teaching role at Becker CPA, remarked to her that "you know I make my living as a teacher." It was said in half-joking manner because this was not the sort of gathering in which one would find a schoolteacher. For her part, Golda did not miss a beat and retorted with "You better watch out, they might make you prime minister."

On another occasion, this one at the White House in March 1979 to celebrate the signing of the Camp David Accords between Israel and Egypt, Rochelle remembers remarking to Newt with the Egyptian president Anwar Sadat within earshot, "I sure hope it sticks"—which shows that Newt was not the only one in the Becker household with political savvy and a healthy sense of foreboding. Today, nearly thirty-five years after the signing, many people are worrying about the same issue and not necessarily liking the odds.

During that gala affair, Newt and Rochelle danced in the ballroom while the famous Marine Corps Band played. It must have been quite a scene and Rochelle turned to Newt with an acknowledgment of how far both had traveled—and here we are not talking about the cross-country journey from California. "Can you believe that the son of a seamstress and the daughter of a butcher are dancing where all the presidents dance?"

Being VIPs at the White House was not the only honor extended to the Beckers. As Rochelle related to me, they traveled to Israel for the funerals of three Israeli prime ministers, Golda Meir, Menachem Begin, and Yitzhak Rabin.

Newt with Pope John Paul II (~1984)

Sometimes, Newt's position as a Jewish and Zionist leader and the responsibilities that came along with the job conflicted with his deeply held convictions. Once, in Israel, he was invited to a meeting where none other than Yasser Arafat, chairman of the Palestine Liberation Organization, would be in attendance. Arafat had more Jewish blood on his hands than anyone since Hitler. In the 1990s, with the signing of the Oslo Agreement, he had seemingly undergone one of the most stunning transformations in the annals of human history. Rehabilitated by the Western media as well as the Israeli government, he was hailed as a peace partner.

Newt, Prime Minister Shimon Peres, Rochelle (~1986)

Arafat was known for speaking in two ways: he spoke of peace and olive branches to the Western people and press, and of hatred and destruction to the Arabic people and press. This was one of the reasons why Newt felt that MEMRI was so important, so that it could expose the words of those like Arafat who could charm the naive with platitudes that made him sound like Gandhi. But now at a meeting where Arafat would be present, proper protocol would indicate that he shake the PLO leader's hand, just as every Israeli prime minister had done since the Oslo Accords, and as every other person in attendance was likely to do. But how could Newton Becker, a man so shaken by the Holocaust, shake the hand of not only a murderer of Jewish children but the acknowledged father of modern terrorism? Newt could not bring himself to shake Arafat's hand, but also being mindful of his leadership role, and ever respectful, he did not want this slight to be noticed by those present. So, with everyone shaking Arafat's hand, Newt headed toward the back door, but was immediately stopped by some official. "You can't leave that way. Don't you want to shake Arafat's hand?" Newt just smiled, and the guy went around the corner expecting Newt to join him. As you can imagine, Arafat was so busy schmoozing with his newfound friends and they with him that Newt was able to make his way out the front door without anyone noticing his flight and his slight. He was a lot more fortunate than others who were not in a position to sneak out a back door or the front door when dealing with Arafat. Such a list is not restricted to Jews, Israelis, or even Americans or Westerners. One remembers the description of General Ion Mihai Pacepa, a former two-star general in Romania's Intelligence Service who had a lot of contact with Arafat in the 1970s, while helping facilitate cooperation and planning between the PLO and the KGB. In his memoir, he recalls, "I felt a compulsion to take a shower whenever I had been kissed by Arafat, or even just shaken his hand."

In the world of Israel advocacy, where he was a veritable giant, you will not find Newt's name or the Becker name on very much at all. Certainly not on any edifice. For all the money he gave—and he was described to me by one person as the most generous Jew in America and by another as giving money away as if he was a billionaire—he was totally uninterested in having his name attached to much. In addition to

Rochelle, Barbara and President George H.W. Bush, Newt at the White House Hanukah party (1991)

Rochelle, Newt and Vice President Al Gore (~1998)

For Rochelle and Newton Becker
with best wishes,
Al Gore

no Becker buildings, you will be hard pressed to find a Becker lecture series, a Becker endowed chair, or a Becker plaque. Newt was never one to seek attention or to advertise his connections. Where did he then find the satisfaction in his giving? To him the acknowledgment of his deeds did not transpire as a result of looking at his name, either in bronze or on paper, but in seeing the results of his work that he could measure in a quantitative way that only an accountant would fully appreciate.

NEWT AND YOUNG PEOPLE

I don't know what Newt thought of George Bernard Shaw's famous aphorism, "Youth is wasted on the young," but he thought this group vitally important if Jewish survival was to be assured. During my first meeting with Newt, one of the things he said was that among all of the organizations he had a major hand in starting, one that he was extremely proud of was initiated through the auspices of the Jewish Federation of Los Angeles. Was it an Israel advocacy or a social welfare organization, I wondered. No, it was a Jewish singles group. It stunned me, but it shouldn't have. Newt had found that in the largely unconnected community of Los Angeles, young Jewish men and women were having difficulty meeting each other. Ultimately, this was not an organization that he started so that young people could have a good time. It was a matter of Jewish survival. And it was also basic accounting. For if these single young Jewish men and women cannot meet, they cannot marry. And marriage leads to children. And without Jewish children, we can have no viable Jewish future. And Newt was all about Jewish survival. Hence, he was not averse to starting

*Senator John Kerry
and Newt (~2002)*

*Newt, Rochelle and Senator
Joe Lieberman (~2004)*

and funding a group whose purpose was social. One suspects that every marriage and every child born of such marriages brought him great satisfaction.

Ironically, for a man who started a social organization, Newt was hardly Mr. Social himself. He could definitely speak to people about a variety of topics and was interested in so much but he did not enjoy small talk or casual conversation and didn't make time for it. He preferred to spend whatever social time he was allocated or which was foisted upon him with family and close friends and generally would attend functions only if there was some larger philanthropic purpose behind it. One person I interviewed spoke to me of Newt's dislike of a certain kind of conversation, one that is never in short supply: "Newt, more than anything, hated BS and would not put up with it." Such is the price to be paid for having a mind and a heart that is preoccupied with the survival of the Jewish people, Israel, and Western civilization. Not only did he not want to hear BS from anyone, he also was not looking to be flattered. He wanted it straight, and he eschewed using his position as a funder to lord anything over anyone. Rather than looking for someone to tell him how wonderful he was, he was more interested in building up others. He was known to compliment someone frequently in an organization who had done a particularly good job at something, knowing this would only encourage that person This was particularly true when he was dealing with young people, a group whom he put so much of his effort into developing. At the end of a long phone conversation about a strategic or organizational matter he would say in a grandfatherly way, "I am really proud of you." It gives one a sense of just what he put into developing and mentoring people and how strong was his connection with them.

One of his first experiences with young people was in his funding of pro-Israel student programs on college campuses. This funding helped set up AIPAC chapters at various universities and allowed student leaders to attend AIPAC conferences. He realized that if you want to create a whole generation of Jewish activists, you have to get them when they are at their idealistic peak. You have to get them in college.

Steve Rosen remembers one of Newt's college outreach programs:

> I worked on the AIPAC College Guide, and Newt personally paid for two hundred thousand to be printed, enough for every Jewish college student in America. It was a huge gift. He gave us the copies and said, "Go find a way to distribute them." We gave them to every Hillel in America. It was Newt's way of fighting back against what Israel's detractors were doing on the campuses. It was classic Newt Becker, extremely well thought out and planned— a brilliant strategy. And he didn't care about the size of the check that it took to get all of this done. It was a huge check, and no one would have dreamed of giving numbers like that at the time. AIPAC's biggest donors that year did not give that much. And this sum Newt gave for one program.

Newt knew the long odds that advocates of Israel faced on the campus, and when he met Lana Becker (no relation) in 1987, while she was still a student herself, he found someone who shared more than just his last name. He found someone who was passionate about Israel and about strengthening support for Israel and Jewish identity on campus. He personally underwrote a project that Lana was passionate about, the writing of a book called a *Guide to Jewish Student Leadership*. It was all very well done and in a how-to catalog style that had first been advanced by the *Whole Earth Catalog* in the late 1960s. It is chockfull of practical advice and enough detail and action steps to make a hands-on accountant like Newt happy.

Influencing young minds on college campuses meant not only organizing students, but also organizing those who influence students, namely their professors. As usual, Newt was a trailblazer in all of this, initially setting up a professors program at AIPAC that brought prominent professors into the Israel advocacy orbit interacting with policy makers and others. In 2005, he phoned Ed Beck, a psychologist and professor who had caught his attention through an organization that he was president of, Scholars for Peace in the Middle East.

For a period of time, Newt played a major role, not only in funding but in helping Scholars for Peace in the Middle East (SPME) utilize the Internet and other resources. As was typical of Newt when he was involved in an organization like SPME, he was focused on how to make it better; as a layperson he delved into areas that were normally reserved for professional staff.

We mentioned Newt's early recognition of the power of technology. He embraced computers early on. Fax machines were something else he championed. This was in the 1980s and well before the explosion of electronic mail. While most organizations would buy one central fax machine, Newt insisted that fax machines be installed in every department. Of course, he put his money where his mouth was and underwrote the entire purchase. Again, he saw the practical and the strategic aspects of it all. Most importantly, you could get a message to multiple people with a group fax and that helped build the urgency of political advocacy. The fax was also a great help in overseas communication, especially in Israel. Likewise, when websites came into vogue, Newt pushed many organizations to set up their first websites and connected them to his favorite web designer. Ever the advocate to use innovative technology to make an organization more effective and more efficient, he saw the benefits of making the most of what's available as soon as it is.

Newt stood behind many Israel Advocacy organizations. Newt had met Jennifer Mizrahi at an AIPAC Policy conference while she was still an undergraduate. While enjoying a successful career in the political and policy arena, she decided that something needed to be done about improving the relationship between the media and Israel. Initially, she approached AIPAC, but it did not want to expand itself into media. It was a politically charged enough task that the Jewish Federation system also took a pass on it, and so with Newt's encouragement as well as others, she decided to start the organization herself. Though she has recently left the organization's helm, in less than a decade she had managed to build a rather large and effective organization: The Israel Project.

This brings us to a very important aspect of Newt. Though he was one of the early forces behind AIPAC, and though he believed that AIPAC was the most important single organization, he saw AIPAC as just one part of an overall Israel Advocacy picture. He saw other groups as complementary to one another like The Israel Project; CAMERA, which focused on anti-Israel bias in the media; JINSA; and StandWithUs, a Los Angeles–based organization set up by Roz Rothstein after 9/11, which has had a large impact on campuses countering anti-Israel propaganda, and operates in other capacities, as well. Newt always sought to lessen competition and turf battles among these organizations. This was one of the biggest contributions he made to the field of Israel advocacy, that is, encouraging and facilitating collaboration among organizations and experts. Given the nature of the competition for funding and status, this was not an easy task, but Newt was unrelenting in this mission. He kept his eyes on the prize and encouraged others to do likewise.

While he still held court at the policy conferences, Newt's role at AIPAC diminished over the years as the organization attracted a whole new group of donors and activists and he focused his attention on so many of these more niche-oriented start-ups. Someone I spoke to described Newt as the Johnny Appleseed of Israel advocacy, so interested was he in helping start or becoming involved early on in worthwhile ways to help. In this, he was akin to being a venture capitalist, which as we saw in the last chapter, he very much was. He was someone always on the lookout for new and improved methods and was excited about being on the cutting edge. As for the risk of some failure that goes along with innovation and being the "first in" on a project, he simply saw this, to use an accounting term, as a "cost of doing business."

CHAPTER EIGHT

September 11th, *The True Believer,* and Defending Democracy

September 11th, 9/11, the attack on the Twin Towers. Whatever name you give it, everyone over a certain age has the date of September 11, 2001 seared in his or her collective memory. Like December 7, 1941, it is a date that is etched in infamy. Lives were lost, lives were changed, a new enemy was introduced, and one thing was clear: the United States would never be the same again.

Where was Newton D. Becker that morning? For Newt it was already afternoon on that dreadful day, and he was traveling by train in the tunnel that connects England to France. He was with Yigal Carmon and as they entered France, Yigal received a phone call informing him about the first plane, and, while they were talking, his colleague started screaming,

"Another one, another one!" That news made any possibility that this was not a terrorist attack out of the question.

That Newt was with Yigal Carmon, the founder of the Middle East Media Research Institute (MEMRI), on that date is a testament to how aware he was of the dangers that the West was facing from Radical Islam. The two men had met at an AIPAC Policy Conference several years earlier just as Yigal was forming the organization. Though they would become very close, the two men came from very different backgrounds. Yigal was raised in and committed to the socialist ideal that had helped build the state of Israel. He had been an officer in the Israel Defense Forces who reached the rank of colonel in his twenty-year career. Fluent in Arabic, Yigal had gained significant expertise in Arab affairs during the period while serving in the IDF and as a counterterrorism adviser to two Israeli prime ministers.

Yigal Carmon is one of those people, sadly in short supply, with no agenda except the truth. He believes that there actually is such a thing as objective truth. In trying to help the public and policy makers better understand the Islamic world and the Middle East, he felt it was imperative for Westerners and their governments to have access, on a real time basis, to what is being said in the Arab and other Middle Eastern media. To do that, of course, is primarily an investment in human capital. More specifically, this required translators and analysts with the requisite expertise, and, you guessed it, no political agendas. Though their original language of interest was Arabic, they now translate sources in Persian, Turkish, Urdu-Pashto, and Dari. That is only one side of the equation, for in addition to translating into English, they have also translated some materials into French, German, Hebrew, Italian, Spanish, Polish, Russian, Chinese, and Japanese.

How did Newt fit into all of this? Newt had bought into Yigal's vision of building an organization to work in this groundbreaking area and had become an early funder of MEMRI. Until his death, he was its largest funder, and Yigal long considered the two close partners in building it up. It was perhaps Newt's greatest achievement in philanthropy. With 9/11, the three-year-old organization would become a critical player as its translations would reach the hallowed halls of Congress, the Pentagon, the Central Intelligence Agency, and nearly every government body or NGO that was interested in what was being said, written about, or blogged in the Middle East.

Why, as an advocate and as one whose primary activity had been political action, was Newt so attracted to the work of an organization that was essentially informational? I posed that question to Yigal, and he told me that Newt understood that information and the mass dissemination thereof could be even more important than an advocacy project. Once one has complete fluency in the information, then one can advocate. It also appears that another feature that attracted Newt to MEMRI was its global reach. No one understood more than Newt that action cannot be restricted to the United States and Israel. MEMRI offered the opportunity to wake up the world to the stark reality that it was facing.

Back to 9/11. Yigal and Newt were supposed to spend two days together in Paris, but, due to the inability to get a flight out, they ended up spending a full week, walking down the Champs-Élysées all the while talking about the upcoming war that the West was facing. Before the planes hit the Twin Towers, the two had been in London, and the discussion mostly centered on a worsening Egyptian situation and the built-in incitement to hate. A few days later, however, the two spoke of Wahhabism, Saudi Arabia, and the world of terror that had seemingly grown out of it, encapsulated as it was in the person of Osama Bin Laden. It was a whole new ballgame.

It was all a great revelation for Newt. He kept saying to himself, "America believes Saudi Arabia is a friend. Americans believe the Saudis are our friends." At some point during those seven days in Paris, Newt had made up his mind that he was going to do everything within his power to fight against the forces that had attacked his country. Though he would call the organizations that fight against extremism "Democracy Defense Organizations" or "DDOs," Newt Becker was readying himself to fight his own version of what became known as the war on terror. His was to be a war of ideas, a war for the truth.

The attacks on 9/11 shocked Americans. Though some of us were aware of the attacks in the previous decade, the first World Trade Center bombing, the USS Cole, and the Embassy bombings in Africa, most of us were pretty unconcerned. The 1990s were, after all, a boom time of hot Internet stocks and a skyrocketing Dow Jones Average. It was a period in which the Soviet Union had fallen and we were all enjoying a well-deserved peace dividend. Any time someone tried to bring up issues of national security and a growing global threat of terrorism, he was almost uniformly hushed up. When such issues were brought into the election of 1996, they were considered laughable. "It's the economy, stupid!" was the popular mantra of the time. It was easy to forget all about the world and its dangers in those prosperous days.

Newt Becker was, as he had always been, going against the stream. He had long fretted over the dangers of terrorism even before the first World Trade Center bombing. One of the things that had caught his attention was a documentary film that came out after that terrible event, which was produced by Steve Emerson. Emerson had an unusual background having worked for Senator Frank Church on the Senate Foreign Relations Committee. He also spent a good number of years as a working journalist for the *New Republic*, *US News and World Report*, and Cable News Network. He had become increasingly alarmed by the level of radical activity in Islam, both in word and in deed.

While we picture radical activity occurring in some remote mountain region of the Near East or being deeply embedded in the sands of Arabia, Emerson was able to witness some pretty harsh stuff on American soil. He heard Islamic radicals calling for acts of violence against America and Israel. The footage that he gathered, much of it clandestinely, became the material for the 1994 documentary that was aired on the PBS award-winning Frontline series, "Terrorists Among Us: Jihad in America."

Newt contacted Steve Emerson, and, like so many of the people whom Newt helped, the two became fast friends and Newt became an early financial supporter in what would eventually become The Investigative Project on Terrorism. In one of the most chilling moments of the documentary, Emerson had stood at the Twin Towers, and we are talking 1994 here, and proclaimed, "The survivors of the explosion of the World Trade Center are still suffering from the trauma, but as far as everyone else is concerned, all this was a spectacular news event that is over. Is it indeed over? The answer is: apparently not. A network of Muslim extremists is committed to a jihad against America. Their ultimate aim is to establish a Muslim empire."

For many Americans, 9/11 was their first taste of the terrible specter of terrorism. What Israel had been experiencing since its inception now looked to be the fate of America. Many Americans were asking questions: Why did they target us? What kind of people are capable of such barbarism? It was a tough thing to get your arms around, but Newt had long had help in understanding fanaticism of various stripes. The assistance came from a man he never knew: Eric Hoffer.

THE TRUE BELIEVER

Anyone who knew Newton Becker well, and particularly grantees, associate Eric Hoffer (known to many as the longshoreman philosopher) with Newt. Hoffer's classic book, *The True Believer: Thoughts on the Nature of Mass Movements*, was more than just a favorite book of Newt's over many decades. It was fundamental to his worldview. In my first meeting with Newt, he asked me if I had ever read Hoffer, and when I responded in the affirmative, it brought a smile to his face. In truth, it had been nearly thirty years since I had read *The True Believer*, but I promised Newt that I would reread the book with fresh eyes. He made it clear that he would hold me to my word.

It is hard to know exactly when Newt first became so attached to this classic. We can verify that it goes back to the 1970s, and perhaps much earlier. *The True Believer* was published in 1951 and received the best kind of publicity when President Eisenhower mentioned it in a national address several years later. Perhaps Newt caught this article penned by Hoffer that appeared in the *Los Angeles Times* on May 26, 1968.

Israel Stands Alone

The Jews are a peculiar people: things permitted to other nations are forbidden to the Jews.

Other nations drive out thousands, even millions of people and there is no refugee problem. Russia did it, Poland and Czechoslovakia did it. Turkey drove out a million Greeks and Algeria a million Frenchmen. Indonesia threw out heaven knows how many Chinese—and no one says a word about refugees.

But in the case of Israel, the displaced Arabs have become eternal refugees. Everyone insists that Israel must take back every single Arab. Arnold Toynbee calls the displacement of the Arabs an atrocity greater than any committed by the Nazis.

Other nations when victorious on the battlefield dictate peace terms. But when Israel is victorious, it must sue for peace. Everyone expects the Jews to be the only real Christians in this world.

Other nations, when they are defeated, survive and recover but should Israel be defeated it would be destroyed. Had Nasser triumphed last June [1967], he would have wiped Israel off the map, and no one would have lifted a finger to save the Jews.

No commitment to the Jews by any government, including our own, is worth the paper it is written on. There is a cry of outrage all over the world when people die in Vietnam or when two Negroes are executed in Rhodesia. But when Hitler slaughtered Jews no one remonstrated with him.

The Swedes, who are ready to break off diplomatic relations with America because of what we do in Vietnam, did not let out a peep when Hitler was slaughtering Jews. They sent Hitler choice iron ore, and ball bearings, and serviced his troop trains to Norway.

The Jews are alone in the world. If Israel survives, it will be solely because of Jewish efforts. And Jewish resources.

Yet at this moment, Israel is our only reliable and unconditional ally. We can rely more on Israel than Israel can rely on us. And one has only to imagine what would have happened last summer had the Arabs and their Russian backers won the war to realize how vital the survival of Israel is to America and the West in general.

I have a premonition that will not leave me; as it goes with Israel so will it go with all of us. Should Israel perish, the Holocaust will be upon us.

Israel must live!

It was not unusual for Newt to quote from the text of *The True Believer* during a conversation. I wanted to know why Newt was so taken by Hoffer and more particularly by the book that had made the longshoreman famous. Steve Rosen posited that the book, and Hoffer's thesis, help explain the three major political mass movements of Newt's lifetime, "Nazism, Communism, and Radical Islam." When I ran this notion of the connection of the three movements by Dr. Richard Pipes, perhaps the leading expert on the Soviet Union who had assigned *The True Believer* to his students at Harvard, he explained that "Hoffer works well to explain any mass movement." Indeed it does.

The connection among Communism, Nazism, and Radical Islam in this spectrum was pointed out by the scholar and writer, Tom Bethell, who recently penned a biography of Hoffer. In the *Longshoreman Philosopher*, Bethell addresses the connection.

> *"Until recently, The True Believer resembled a piece of theoretical machinery that lacked an application more recent than the 'Hitler decade.' Hoffer assumed that he was living in a godless age, and the discussion of mass movements and true believers seemed more relevant to an earlier time. There were a few mentions of Islam in the book, but in the mid-twentieth century that faith was hibernating, at least in terms of its impact on the West. But a remarkable feature of The True Believer is that the Islamist revival, unforeseen when the book was written, confirmed Hoffer's ideas in detail.*
>
> *With the September 11, 2001 terrorist attacks on New York and Washington, The True Believer was rushed back into print. Jihadists seemed to be following Hoffer's old script. Young men were joining the Islamist cause with little in the way of coercion, volunteering for death in return for promised rewards in the afterlife.*
>
> *Mass movements deprecate the present, Hoffer wrote in* The True Believer, *by depicting it as a mean preliminary to a glorious future. The hope released by the visualization of such a future is a most potent source of a daring self-forgetting. Dying or killing seem easy when they are a part of a ritual, ceremonial, dramatic performance or*

game. The leader of such a movement has to promote a devil—ideally a foreigner—and he has to evoke in his followers the illusion that they are participating in a grandiose spectacle.

The conditions that generate true believers, in Hoffer's analysis, are conspicuous in the Arab world. The Islamist revival has shown that the book doesn't belong to a particular time or place."

This definitely seems to be a key to Newt's attraction to Hoffer. But even with such a well-reasoned argument one could not help but think there was even more to Newt's attraction to Hoffer to consider.

It was Eleanor Roosevelt who famously noted that "Great minds discuss ideas; average minds discuss events; small minds discuss people." Hoffer was known not only as a man of ideas, but a lover of ideas. Newt's mind was likewise occupied with the world of ideas. Hoffer was also a great generalizer of ideas. When Newt would speak about the Middle East, democracy, freedom, and anything big, it was his way to generalize.

We have spent considerable time speaking about the central role that Zionism has played in Newt's life and world view. In reading the piece that Hoffer wrote about Israel, "Israel Stands Alone," it is obvious how important Israel was to Hoffer. When interviewed by CBS's Eric Sevareid shortly before the Six Day War, Hoffer was asked if America, in the wake of whatever assistance it has rendered Israel, has not repaid its debt for lack of assistance during the Holocaust. Hoffer responded that this is a debt that can never be repaid, that the lack of taking in Jewish refugees and sending some back to what would be their deaths, is something that America will have to live with and confers an unlimited obligation to help Israel. He states in the "Israel Stands Alone" piece, "I have a premonition that will not leave me; as it goes with Israel so will it go with all of us. Should Israel perish, the Holocaust will be upon us." This is very similar to the concept that Newt was vehement about in the post-9/11 era: Israel is the "canary in the mine shaft" was something Newt would constantly speak about and passionately believed in.

American Exceptionalism is another area in which Newt would find common cause with Hoffer. Not only is Hoffer out to explain the appeal of totalitarianism and the ever danger-ous mass movement, he contrasts it with what he sees as the healthiest political system, our own republic. Not only is it the healthiest political system, but the healthiest economic sys-tem, one that could allow a longshoreman to become a best-selling author and foster a climate whereby a poor kid from Glenville, Ohio ends up a multi-millionaire.

Hoffer explores the irrationality that leads to *The True Believer*. He places his own hopes for a better world in the power of rational thinking. Newt shared those sentiments. Rationality seemed to pervade everything that was Newton Becker, from Becker CPA, to his investments, down to his phi-lanthropy. It was Yigal Carmon who pointed out that "Newt's unshakable belief in rationality verged on naivete. He was cer-tain that all problems could be solved with the right approach, analysis, and treatment."

In March 2012, two months after Newt passed away, Rochelle Becker accepted an award for Newt on behalf of an organization that he helped found, the European Leadership Network, known as ELNET, which we will turn our attention

Newt and Rochelle giving President Jimmy Carter a book
*that appears to be **The True Believer** (~1980)*

to shortly. All those in attendance at Hillcrest Country Club received a copy of *The True Believer*. It was not the first time that Newt had given out copies of his favorite book. He had given them to politicians and to many of the grantees and the staffs of the organizations in which he played a major role. He gave them to friends and to family. He may have been the single biggest factor in keeping up interest in *The True Believer* before 9/11 that is, until as Tom Bethell mentioned, interest was renewed in the classic. That it never waned for Newt is obvious. But he took advantage of the times, and felt it imperative that every member of the U.S. Congress have a copy of the book, and, he hoped, read it.

There was only one problem with Newt's plan. By 2002, the only copies of *The True Believer* still in print were paperbacks. Newt felt them insufficiently formal for the intended audience, and so with the publisher, had a large group of books printed in hardcover format with an elegant dust jacket included. It was hardly an inexpensive venture, but for Newt Becker it was well worth the cost and the effort. President Eisenhower, who had tried to get them in the hands of as many influential people as possible during his years as president, would have been proud.

The edition printed by Newt in 2002

These were three of Newt's favorite quotes from *The True Believer* that he often cited:

"Hatred is the most accessible and comprehensive of all unifying agents [for mass movements]. . . . Mass movements can rise and spread without belief in a God, but never without belief in a devil. Usually the strength of a mass movement is proportionate to the vividness and tangibility of its devil." (p. 91)

"A movement is pioneered by men of words, materialized by fanatics and consolidated by men of action. It is usually an advantage to a movement, and perhaps a prerequisite for its endurance, that these roles should be played by different men succeeding each other as conditions require." (p. 147)

"The man of action saves the movement from the suicidal dissensions and the recklessness of the fanatics. But his appearance usually marks the end of the dynamic phase of the movement. The war with the present is over. The genuine man of action is intent not on renovating the world but on possessing it. Whereas the life breath of the dynamic phase was protest and a desire for drastic change, the final phase is chiefly preoccupied with administering and perpetuating the power won." (p. 149)

THE EUROPEAN CHALLENGE

Newt was known to ask questions when he already had the answer at the ready. He often pointed out that in public opinion polls taken in the United States, when the question is asked, "Whom do you favor in the current dispute between the Israelis and the Palestinians?" Americans favor the Jewish State by a 3 to 1 margin. The opposite is true in France. There the number is 3 to 1 in favor of the Palestinians. In England the number is 2 to 1 in favor of the Palestinians, and, in Germany, the citizenry is evenly divided. The question that Newt then posed was "Why is there such a dramatic difference between Europe and America?"

I thought Newt was testing me to see how aware I was of these issues, and so I went through a whole litany: first, the geopolitical concerns that we alluded to earlier when speaking about the Six Day War, then the larger percentage of the American population who were Evangelical Christians and Christian Zionists. America has no entrenched history of anti-Semitism, no expulsions, pogroms, massacres, and no Holocaust. From there I went on to talk about the identification that the Puritan founders had with the ancient Israelites, how a few even spoke about making Hebrew an official language. Oh, and America did not have the Muslim population of Europe, and Europe did not have the Jewish population of the United States. I still had plenty more arguments left in me when Newt suddenly cut me off. "No, those may be true, but the most important reason that Europe is not as pro-Israel as America is that Europe does not have an AIPAC or other pro-Israel organizations." It was quite a statement, and I knew that as a major force behind AIPAC, Newt was partial. I also got the distinct impression that he had heard my arguments before, and, while he agreed, to Newt Becker, they were beside the point.

"Some men see things as they are and wonder why. I dream of things that never were and wonder why not." We first mentioned George Bernard Shaw's quote in an earlier chapter and it seems to capture something of the spirit of Newton D. Becker. It was Newt who thought that the difference between Europe and America was having AIPAC and other pro-Israel organizations. Rather than just analyze the situation and bemoan it, Newt went about trying to rectify it. He spent considerable energy in the last decade of his life trying to build these organizations in Europe. It was to be one of his last great undertakings.

Newt may have been thinking about Europe for a long time, but the events of the Second Intifada of the Palestinians that started in the fall of 2000, brought it to the fore. Europe was taking a harshly anti-Israel direction in response to Palestinian propaganda and biased reporting. Jews in many countries were made deeply uncomfortable by the climate of hostility toward Israel and Jews. In France, a poll showed that 20% of Jews were *seriously considering* emigrating. Something had to be done.

So Newt, knowing that there needed to be organizations standing up for Israel in Europe, took a trip there to see what had to be done. As David Becker said, "I was very proud of my father. I saw him as a sort of modern day Theodore Herzl, traveling all over Europe to drum up support for a new way of thinking about Israel and European Jewry's role." Newt was objecting to what he saw as a traditional tendency for European Jews to keep their heads down and hope that troubles would pass. He was trying to get people to take action. He met with the few people who were involved in advocacy and with potential donors. He urged them to expand existing organizations and to create new ones. He offered matching funds to motivate giving, and made the case, "If I, an American Jew who has no business connections and no family connections here is willing to contribute to this, shouldn't you do it as well? This is your home and your life. You can invest a little money now to fight for your place in this country or you may lose a fortune if you're forced to leave. If you increase what you're going to give, I will match your increase." This had a big impact.

A major step took place in 2003. Newt and Larry Hochberg invited a group of about seventy-five leaders from Europe and some other countries, professionals from existing organizations and potential donors, to Washington for a special program organized and run by Newt and Larry around the AIPAC annual policy conference. It would give them an opportunity to see what Israel advocacy American style was all about and spend time with AIPAC staffers and dedicated, strategic thinkers like Newt Becker and Larry Hochberg. Newt and Larry also organized a second program for the following year. In addition, Newt continued traveling to Europe to build contacts with European philanthropists. The level of giving on the continent had never been up to the standards in the United States, and Newt felt this needed to change if anything would ever happen.

In Europe, there already were some pro-Israel organizations in place, but they were poorly funded and largely ineffective. As the new initiative was coming around, Newt found out that the largest European donor was giving an overly modest amount. He knew that such amounts were vastly insufficient to build what was necessary and he did not want the Europeans to be dependent on American money. He told the European leader that he would double the amount the man had given the previous years, provided that he would match it. He did. He was also trying to break certain attitudes that Europeans had toward lobbying and assuage their fears that their activities would be viewed as Jews try-ing to "buy" the foreign policy of their country. (Newt knew that this canard had long tried to gain traction among both the extreme Left and the extreme Right.)

Not every meeting with European Jewish leaders went well. As we have described, Newt did not mince words. At times, he almost lectured very powerful men on the importance of politi-cal advocacy and on the need for wealthy Jews to contribute to that effort. Not all of these men took to the message or to the messenger, but some did, and Newt kept plugging away.

Newt had long thought that it might not be appropriate for AIPAC to lead the European initiative. AIPAC's mission is focused on the relationship between America and Israel, and involving other countries was potentially problematic. Also, it is, after all, a mammoth organization with a lot to worry about, and he feared that the European initiative would fall by the wayside. Newt eventually came to the realization that a new organization had to be built.

Newt was one who frequently went it alone. But for the organization that would become the European Leadership Network, he partnered with his good friend and fellow philan-thropist, Larry Hochberg. Larry shared much in common with Newt. They both began their philanthropic lives in a Federa-tion setting, were both native Midwesterners, both business innovators, and both largely saw eye to eye on Israel and geo-political issues.

In 2007, ELNET began with an office in Brussels and would eventually operate in many countries. Raanan Eliaz was the founding director, Larry Hochberg the founding president, and they hired staff to raise money and support the efforts of their European partners. Though the story has yet to be written, from all accounts, after all the hard work put in so far, their efforts seem to be paying off.

European philanthropists were not the only ones Newt was speaking to about the importance of advocacy. He had long felt that his American colleagues, despite their overwhelming support for AIPAC, were slow at embracing the concept of "perimeter organizations" and what he would call "democracy defense organizations." The coining of those terms seemed to come about in the period after 9/11.

NEWT'S FUNDING STRATEGY

Newt understood the need to fund strategically. He pointed out that no matter how much the Jewish community and others funded Democracy Defense Organizations, the Saudis, with their vast oil wealth, could always outspend us. This led him to think about optimizing every dollar spent.

Nir Boms met Newt shortly after 9/11 at an AIPAC policy conference. This seemingly chance encounter would affect the lives of both of them. Nir was working for the Foundation for Defense of Democracies, a group founded by Cliff May after 9/11, and Newt was asked to serve on its board. Newt would eventually ask Nir to work for the Newton and Rochelle Becker Charitable Trust, and they began a period of sustained collaboration—and, as occurred with so many people Newt worked with, friendship.

Nir explained how the term *perimeter* and much of the lexicon Newt began to use came into being.

"We spoke often in those days, the days of the second intifada, of the 'War on Terror' and of the war in Iraq. The

vision of peace had slipped further away and the politi-
cal arena was already beating the drums of war. The per-
ceived reality was shaped, in the case of Palestinians and
Israelis, by pundits and commentators who often confused
villains and victims. If the media served as a barometer,
then Israel and the Jewish people appeared to be losing
that war—and this is where Newt stepped in. "We must
support organizations that can speak to policy makers
using a broader perspective. These groups are our defense
assets: think tanks and advocacy groups that operate in
the centers of decision making in order to create a better
public understanding of the reality of the Middle East."

Newt thought that the American Jewish philanthropic community should not focus exclusively on its internal problems:
Jewish education, social welfare, and the like. It must also support organizations that are on its perimeter and interact with
non-Jewish audiences, particularly with those audiences that
impact the community and Israel such as policy makers and
the news media.

On October 9, 2003, Newt gave a presentation to other LA-
based philanthropists. The purpose was to try to increase their
giving to perimeter organizations. Newt defined the perimeter organizations this way: Perimeter organizations protect
the Jewish community by interfacing and interacting with
the government and society of the country we live in. Perimeter organizations are involved in fighting a 'War of Words'
by supplying information to different constituencies (policy
makers, opinion leaders, and the public) in support of Western democratic values in the Middle East and to counter bias
against Israel. He suggested that each person give 20% of his

charitable giving to these kinds of organizations and provided a list of organizations that he thought were effective.

Newt especially appreciated those organizations that engaged in the "War of Words" and that fought back against "lies, half-truths, and gross exaggerations"—a phrase he often used. He specifically rejected the approach advocated by some, especially in Europe, that it is best to stay quiet and let the harsh words blow over. He believed that "a lie left uncountered, becomes the truth." In other words, it is always necessary to stand up for the truth or risk a lie becoming perceived as reality.

Because of his passion for standing up to the lies, Newt had limited enthusiasm for a certain kind of pro-Israel organization that focused on "Israel beyond the conflict." The philosophy of those groups was to ignore the contentious debates about the Arab-Israeli conflict that they feel lead the public to negative feelings about both sides ("a pox on both their houses") and to try to draw attention to the many positive aspects of Israel, such as its cutting edge high-tech industry and its vibrant arts scene. Newt had nothing against highlighting Israel's virtues; he just felt that his funding was more critically needed to counter the lies, and that those lies were the real danger to the Jewish people—the lies couldn't be ignored.

Newt took the position that the lies, half-truths, and gross exaggerations were intended to demonize Israel and portray it as the evil party. This, of course, would act to undercut the willingness of people to support Israel at times of crisis. The real battle for hearts and minds was being waged in the realm of good vs. evil. Focusing on the latest Israeli high-tech startup or the Tel Aviv nightlife might generate some mild positive feelings when all was quiet, but would be irrelevant when the conflict heated up.

THE HIERARCHY OF IMPACT

Newt realized that there were a number of important audiences who should know the truth about Israel and the Middle East. Over time, this insight evolved into a more systematic view that Newt called "the Hierarchy of Impact." The basic idea is that some people matter more than other people and that a rational allocation of resources should take that into account.

Newt divided the population into three slices: policy makers, opinion leaders, and the public. There are a very small number of policy makers who actually set government policy toward Israel, the Middle East, the Jewish community, and the West generally; it is critically important that they understand the truth about relevant issues. There is a much larger, but still small, group of opinion leaders who are trusted sources of information and whose views affect many more people. They are also very important. Finally, there is the public, most of whom do not care about, or have any influence over, these issues, but who also need to be educated to some extent so that they support, or at least don't object to, the views and policies of the policy makers.

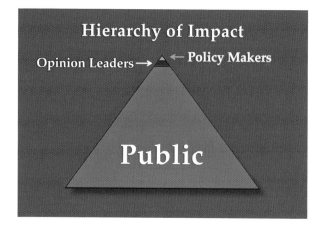

Each of these 3 slices of "the pyramid" could be further divided into different groups. Policy makers could be divided into elected officials and the executive branch including the State Department, Defense Department, and other agencies. What Newt realized is that in most cases, different non-profit organizations focused on different groups. For example, AIPAC focused on elected officials and adopted an approach and style that was appropriate for that group. In contrast, The Washington Institute for Near East Policy, a think tank in Washington, was more focused on participating in the debate in the State Department and the foreign policy-making community of the executive branch in general, and developed an approach and style appropriate for that audience.

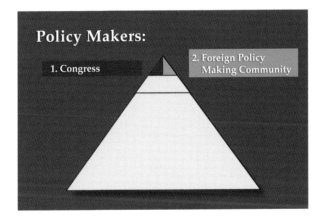

Similarly, the opinion leaders could be divided into different groups, each of which needed its own approach, and usually its own dedicated non-profit organization. Probably the most important opinion leader was the media, and a number of organizations have tried to educate and provide information to reporters and editors, but other key groups include professors, clergy, teachers and textbook publishers. Organizations dealing with these groups were later in coming.

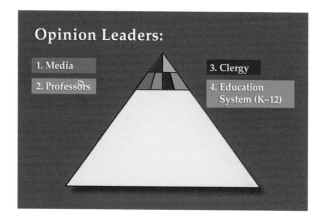

Finally, the public can also be segmented. Some organizations cast a wide net over the general public, but others focus on specific groups such as college students, high school students, Evangelical Christians, Mainline Christians, Muslims, and Jews, as each audience often responds better to a customized approach.

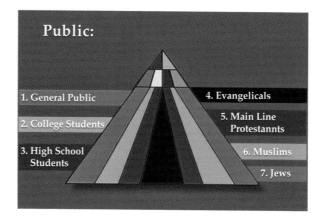

Newt believed that a rational allocation of resources meant that it was justifiable to spend a relatively large amount of money on a per-person basis to educate and influence policy makers because each person was so important. When dealing with the public, however, it only made sense to support programs that had, to use another accounting term, a low "cost per beneficiary." For example, Newt believed that it made perfect sense to spend, say, $9,000 per person to take every congressman to Israel to learn about the country and its issues, but that it did not make sense to spend $3,000 per person to take every college student to Israel. One of these students might grow up to be the next U.S. president, but probably not, and the one congressman's trip was likely to be exponentially more impactful on American policy and the protection of the Jewish people than the trip for the three students.

For organizations that dealt directly with the public, Newt looked for low cost opportunities to reach a lot of people, and when the Internet and websites first became widely used, this provided a wonderful mechanism to do that. For example, he was delighted to support a number of projects that his son, David, initiated for websites in Arabic and Farsi, aimed at the public in the Middle East, that presented accurate information about the Holocaust, the history of Jewish communities in the Arab world, and Israel.

Another way of reaching the public, and one that was often cost-effective, was through the different opinion leaders who influenced the various segments of the public. Some of these opinion leaders also influenced policy makers, to a lesser extent. Newt was a leader in funding and advising organizations that worked with the various opinion leaders and was often one of the first funders of these organizations.

In order to best allocate resources, Nir Boms suggested that they map the field and determine which organizations were active in the different parts of the hierarchy of impact. Newt agreed, and worked with Nir and Gali Cooks, whom Nir recruited to manage the project, to develop criteria for inclusion and to think through the type of information to be collected from each organization. One of the most important pieces of data was the budget of each of the organizations which they could obtain from publicly available tax returns. During 2003 and 2004, they assembled the first draft of a database that allowed them to determine which parts of the hierarchy of impact were being attended to and which ones needed more help. In the years that followed, the database became more sophisticated and included organizations from all over the world.

Getting back to Newt's speech in 2003: Was he successful in convincing the philanthropists in the room to give to perimeter organizations? It is very hard to say and only a study that would have looked at the before and after giving to perimeter organizations by those in attendance would reveal the answer. However, it was not just that Newt *wanted* to see the giving among his fellow philanthropists change, he seemed to have felt a *responsibility* to do so. John Fishel, formerly the number one professional in the Los Angeles Jewish Federation was there for the presentation. He observed Newt engage with a variety of different professionals and philanthropists over the years. He recalls, "Newt would talk to anyone who would listen. He could be dogged but yet very low key. When discussing policy and political matters he would say, 'let me tell you why I believe this, and not you should believe this because. . . .' I never saw him preach but rather he talked with you. Even when people took issue with him, he would say, 'you are wrong. Now let me convince you how you're wrong.' He would then use hard empirical evidence in his argument and when a person still was unconvinced he never let it affect his relationship with that person."

Trying to convince people of his position utilizing evidence and facts and done in a low key way was an obligation that he carried with him 24/7 and had no limiting factors. Rabbi Avraham Berkowitz is Newt's great-nephew, the grandson of his brother, Phil. Rabbi Berkowitz and his brother, Yirmi, also a rabbi who does important work in the United Nations that Newt supported, got to know Newt while still teenagers and spent time with Newt while visiting their grandparents in Los Angeles. Newt had considerable influence on them over the years and when Rabbi Avraham Berkowitz became an emissary of the Chabad Lubavitch movement and was working in Russia, Newt liberally supported the educational, religious and cultural outreach to the Jews of that land.

Once while visiting St. Petersburg and staying in one of the great hotels of that majestic city, Newt and his great-nephew met a prominent Jewish businessman from the Pacific Northwest. The man was a peer of Newt's, and, in addition to having been a partner in a very large enterprise, was a lay leader in communal and Zionist affairs. Newt queried him on where his considerable philanthropic dollars were going and the man, as would be expected, given the statistics that Newt himself used, gave the overwhelming amount of his charity to social welfare activities. Newt began to tell him that he was not using his funds wisely, that unless priorities were shifted to the perimeter organizations that we have spoken about, there would be no future for the Jewish people or Israel. That was the change that his great-nephew noticed throughout Newt's interaction with people, not just with this gentleman: Newt felt that in the post-9/11 world with the extremists out to kill us, philanthropists must work to protect ourselves from the radicals, in addition to building schools and synagogues.

CHAPTER NINE

Mentorship and Continuity

THE SEARCHER

Newt believed in the power of ideas, but he also believed deeply in the power of people. He funded some extremely talented people who shared his dedication to the mission. How, I wonder, did these people and Newt end up in such collaboration? One place he met such like-minded people was at the annual AIPAC Policy Conference where he was, of course, a fixture. He was also contacted occasionally by people who were referred by one of Newt's grantees who was familiar with their work. However, sometimes, as Bryan Gordon explained to me when I posed the question: "You did not find Newt; Newt found you."

* * *

Yaakov Kirschen is the author and illustrator of the "Dry Bones" cartoons. A native New Yorker, he began pursuing his vocation during his student days in New York and continued when he made his way to settle in Israel in the early 1970s. His work was picked up by the Jerusalem Post and he was able to keep body and soul together while engaged in that profession.

By the 1990s, the newspaper business began to change. The success of the Internet started to encroach on many areas of what had exclusively been the purview of print media. Classified advertising took a hit, and, as revenue and subscriptions declined, newspapers could no longer afford to pay for things like cartoons. For Yaakov, it was very much a mixed blessing. With the explosion of the Internet, his cartoons could now be viewed by more people in more places than ever before. The problem with this new media configuration was that a man has to eat. So, in the spirit of the great artists of the Renaissance, Yaakov began looking for a sponsor. He found his Medici when someone who worked for Newt called him. He did not know of Newt and what the person on the other end of the phone said must have surprised him. Yaakov was asking for a certain amount of money. Newt's person asked him if an amount greater than that would not in fact be preferable.

Newt Becker supporting a cartoon? This does not sound like his cup of tea until you hear about the kind of cartoon that Yaakov was drawing. "Dry Bones" was a cartoon that was politically oriented, and one that fused together humor and keen insights into the Middle East. It touched on such matters in a way that the standard op-ed piece could not. Ever the creative thinker himself, Newt appreciated what Yaakov was doing and what such a medium could accomplish. Newt not only began sponsoring Yaakov, but the two became good friends. For years the two spoke on the phone every week

A Dry Bones strip featuring
Yaakov Kirschen's alter ego, Mr. Shuldig.

brainstorming ideas for cartoons. Newt would often high-
light some current event that he knew must have an ironic,
funny angle, but it took Yaacov's out-of-the box comic mind
to find it.

This strip, like many others, was based on real events. Below is a screen shot from a TV episode of the Hamas young children's program, "Pioneers of Tomorrow," when Assud gives his farewell speech in the hospital before dying from Israeli shelling. The Assud bunny character had been introduced to replace his brother, Nahoul the bumblebee, who also "died a martyr's death" less than a year earlier.

DryBonesBlog.com

* * *

Avi Schnurr is as different from Yaakov Kirschen as one could imagine—an engineer and rocket scientist straight out of Central Casting. Avi worked on the original Reagan-era missile defense "Star Wars" program known as SDI (Strategic Defense Initiative).

Missiles and bombs sound plenty serious, but there are different kinds and degrees of threats. At the top of the lethal list is the very real danger that rogue states or terrorists might use an electromagnetic pulse (EMP) produced by a nuclear explosion as a weapon directed at our electric grid. It sounds like something out of a James Bond movie, and, in fact an EMP weapon was featured in the 1995 Bond film "Golden-Eye" (although they got the facts wrong). Such potential has been around for years. While the threat traditionally was from established nuclear powers, most especially the Soviet Union, that concern has now shifted to rogue states like Iran and North Korea which need only one nuclear weapon and a rudimentary delivery system to carry out such an attack.

Although few in the public are aware of the threat of a nuclear EMP attack, a single, ordinary nuclear bomb, if exploded in the upper atmosphere, generates an electromagnetic pulse that, given our current state of unpreparedness, can severely damage or destroy the electrical grid in about one-third of the United States in one blow. Our large populations cannot survive without pumped water, refrigeration, transportation, and communication. Because key elements of the grid would take more than a year to replace, *tens of millions* of people would die from starvation and disease as a result of a single nuclear explosion. The threat is sufficiently

serious that a Congressional commission concluded that only
ten to thirty percent of the U.S. population would survive this
type of attack.

Fortunately, it is relatively easy and cheap (by national
standards) to protect us from this catastrophe. Unfortunately,
industry is stalling and our government is moving at a glacial
pace. That's where Avi Schnurr comes in. Avi founded and
runs the EIS (Electric Infrastructure Security) Council whose
goal is to educate and mobilize the government and the power
industry to take steps to harden the grid to protect against
this threat.

Newt understood the magnitude of this threat. By supporting the EIS Council he thought he was not just contributing
toward saving the Jewish people, but he was also helping save
the American people and all of modern society! When Newt
introduced Avi to others, he would introduce him as the man
"who is saving the world." Avi developed a genuine admiration for Newt: his keen analytic skills, and his unique approach
and perspective. When one is facing an overwhelming mission, as Avi was, it is invaluable to have an ally and supporter
like Newt behind you. Avi describes the difference Newt made
for him: "Miracles are the times when the impossible is set
aside and overcome, and this is one of the many gifts Newt left
us. Newt's gift was to look at a brick wall and see a problem that
would yield to a determined, carefully thought out plan." Most
helpful, too, was "his constant advice, and especially his unwavering confidence that the impossible could be achieved."

* * *

There were others out to heal the world or certainly to make
it a safer place for Israel and the Jewish people. One such

person is Newt's fellow Angeleno, Roz Rothstein. Roz is the child of Holocaust survivors, and, like so many survivors and their families, developed into a passionate and unwavering supporter of Israel. When the Second Intifada began in 2000 with a relentless level of violence against Jews not seen in the Holy Land since the Arab riots of the 1920s and 1930s, many Jews throughout the world wanted to do something in support of the besieged country. They reacted in different ways. Although most Jews were silent, confused, and frozen, some were able to act. There were those who bravely marched in support of their brethren, others who sent money, and still a minority of those who involved themselves in various forms of political advocacy.

There were very few who made such advocacy their primary life focus. Roz Rothstein did not originally venture to make this her life work; she already had a successful career as a psychologist. In 2001 together with her husband, Jerry, she formed StandWithUs whose mission was to mobilize the Jewish community. It started as a local Southern Californian advocacy group stocked strictly with volunteers. Like much of what Newt involved himself in, though, it has grown significantly in geographical reach, staff, budget and impact.

Newt was there at the very beginning. He met Roz at the Hillcrest Country Club where the two attended a meeting with a small number of Los Angeles Jewish leaders to discuss what could be done to support Israel during this terrible time. Both Roz and her husband were deeply outraged by the local and national media coverage of the events in the Middle East. They felt the coverage was heavily biased against the Jewish state and they also felt that the established Jewish leadership lacked both vision and strategy in combatting the latest rash of anti-Israel media activity. The Rothsteins were anxious to take some form of action that would support the Israeli people and were able to procure funding to fly a private plane with a pro-Israel message on Israel Independence Day. They also rented a booth during that day and called it "Israel, we stand with you. Hence, the organization came to be called "StandWithUs." A good number of people remember seeing that plane as a very emotional moment. Many came up to express their support and they signed up for what was to be the fledgling organization's first meeting, an emergency meeting at that, where all interested parties were invited to brainstorm ideas of ways they could support Israel. Talk about grassroots. This was grassroots.

Newt was at that meeting. He came prepared to render support with both ideas and resources. His first piece of advice was to incorporate. His second piece of advice was to become a 501(c)3 corporation so people could donate more freely to what would be a legitimate non-profit organization. His financial support came with a proviso, however: he would support the organization only if it did not limit its activities to California. That it needed to have a national reach illustrates that Newt understood that this was not a local problem. In fact, he later encouraged Roz and Jerry to go international and as of this writing, StandWithUs has branch offices in the UK, Canada, and Israel as well as the USA. Once Newt had Roz' assurance, he wrote a check to help cover the cost of the organization's first booklet. As Roz stated, "Newt's overarching dream was to systematize our work so that it would be easy to export and would reach wide audiences. He wanted to do that with all the groups he mentored and funded. He added so much to our meetings with simple words of encouragement as well as applying his own teaching perspective to make sure that we looked at all ways to make our newest campaigns and projects exportable."

Remember what Professor Sam Edelman called Newt? The Johnny Appleseed of pro-Israel advocacy. Well, by the second year in business, StandWithUs had gotten quite a few people to stand with them and stand with Israel. Some even pulled out their checkbooks. They raised $250,000 and before long the organization had expanded to New York and Detroit. Not only was Newt a strong supporter of the group's annual budget requirements, but he also provided additional funds for special projects.

One of Newt's first funding ventures was a website called "Stand4Facts." It was a resource for profiling Middle East specialist speakers and identifying the "lies, half-truths, and gross exaggerations" in their presentations. This was done where StandWithUs was to make its biggest impact: the university campus. By vetting the speakers, the organization would provide pro-Israel students with the requisite questions which would serve to reveal the speaker's bias. Newt felt that by using only one website (and it required constant work to update), an important niche could be filled in Israel advocacy. Remember that central to Newt's belief in Israel advocacy work was that organizations should not be competing against each other for funds or for publicity. Each should play a unique and vital role, one that would complement the others. Turf wars were counterproductive to the ultimate goal.

Naturally enough, Newt was proud of the organization that StandWithUs became, and proud of the influence he had on it. According to Roz Rothstein, the encouragement and advice that he gave in those early years were every bit as vital as the funding. When Roz spoke of Newt, it was clear the degree to which he was able to motivate and encourage. Roz recounted, "He'd always say, 'You know I want you to do well, I want you to succeed.' When Newt was really happy about something, he'd use the word 'terrific.' He would light up with excitement when he liked an idea."

There was much to be happy about as the organization expanded its reach and grew its budget well into the seven figures. That they were able to succeed with so many other funding sources must have satisfied the Johnny Appleseed in Newt. The organization has had no greater friends or more generous supporters than Newt's friends and fellow philanthropists, Rita and Steve Emerson, of whom we shall soon speak. Most of all, though, Newt Becker was all about results and when it came to StandWithUs he really liked the results for they were faring well in the battle of ideas. When he talked to Roz Rothstein about scaling the operation, he would draw on examples not only from relevant organizations like AIPAC but from his own experiences at Becker CPA.

In many ways, Newt tried to develop the organizations he supported along the model of the Becker CPA Review Course. Newt stressed the importance of mass communication using state-of-the-art technology from fax machines to email, to the Internet. He applied business and marketing strategy to philanthropy and was able to help build organizations all over the world.

Then there was the personal side. Though he was an early supporter and a major figure on the board, it must be mentioned that like so many of Newt's relationships, friendship and personal esteem lay at the heart of his feelings for the Rothsteins. As he cared about his students at Becker CPA, Newt would offer the Rothsteins nutritional advice and share with them his medical insights. He was more than a simply a friend; he was a valued counselor and father figure. Roz Rothstein recounted, "The world has lost a treasure, and I have personally lost a cherished, irreplaceable mentor and friend."

While Israel advocacy and Defense of Democracy captivated Newt and made up his primary area of interest, it was not his sole focus. Given his concern about Jewish survival, he had long been concerned about the effect of intermarriage on the future of the Jewish people. Many years earlier, in the pre-internet age, Newt had founded and supported a Jewish singles service in Los Angeles that utilized the latest high technology of the day—the telephone answering machine with a cassette taped message and a dedicated phone line—to publicize Jewish singles events around town.

By 2004, a large and growing number of Jews had married non-Jews and there was real concern about whether those new families would be part of the Jewish community. So, when Newt met Ed Case, he was interested.

* * *

Ed Case, like Roz, had been engaged in full time work in another arena before starting his non-profit organization, InterfaithFamily. He was, in fact, a lawyer who practiced for twenty-two years with a major firm in Boston before changing directions mid-career by attending Brandeis University where he received a Master's Degree in Jewish Communal Work. He was looking for a niche in the Jewish world and felt that among the most underserved in the community were interfaith couples and their families.

This is clearly a serious issue. According to the latest Pew Research Poll which was conducted in 2013, fully 58%

of American Jews and 71% of non-Orthodox Jews marry someone from another faith. What happens to these couples, what are the resources available to them, how will they find their way in the Jewish world, and how will they handle the challenges associated with holidays and child rearing were just some of the questions and concerns that had confronted Ed Case when he founded InterfaithFamily.

The organization's mission statement is that it is in business to "empower interfaith families to make Jewish choices and to encourage Jewish communities to welcome them." Intriguing stuff to be sure, but how does Newt Becker fit into the picture?

The two met at the United Jewish Communities' General Assembly in November 2004 in Newt's hometown of Cleveland, Ohio. The GA, as it is known to insiders, is an annual gathering of communal leaders, Federation professionals, and philanthropists. Those like Ed who are looking to generate interest and funding from those in attendance set up booths. A curious Newt Becker, who was scouting the booths, soon found himself engaged with Ed and clearly was interested in both the man and the mission. Newt dealt in reality. It was not the 40s and 50s in Cleveland when intermarriage was an anomaly. In part of an e-mail to a prominent Jewish professional whom he asked to help Ed, it was clear what part of Newt's interest was in the organization. Regarding the topic he stated, "I believe the statistics of Jewish intermarriage and the percent going Jewish and the percent going Gentile with the percent in the middle is important. It seems the middle percent is 'up for grabs' and with 'effort' can be salvaged as Jews."

As with Roz Rothstein, Newt shared something of his operating philosophy with Ed, largely culled from his years at the helm of Becker CPA. Rather than just maintain the company as a web-based educational resource, Newt encouraged the organization to open field offices where it could conduct actual programs. Again, Newt emphasized to Ed all of the quality control issues that he had faced at Becker during his expansion phase. This direction is largely the one that the InterfaithFamily has chosen to follow with offices in Boston, Chicago, San Francisco, and Philadelphia. In addition to lending material support and strategic advice, Newt helped open doors allowing Ed to use his name when contacting prospective donors.

* * *

Carice Witte is an American *olah* (immigrant to Israel) who spent a twenty-year career actively engaged in high-tech deals and real estate ventures. Despite her success in business, like Roz and Ed, she yearned to make a difference in something that she was passionate about. She was passionate about two areas and most specifically the intersection of the two: Israel and China. The former grew naturally enough as a result of her upbringing and commitments. The latter passion, for Asia, first came to the fore during her undergraduate years at Yale.

The People's Republic of China and the State of Israel have an interesting history. China, like the Soviet Union, supported left-wing liberation movements which meant supporting the terrorism of the Palestine Liberation Organization as it sought the destruction of the State of Israel. After the death of Chairman Mao and with the normalization of relations with the Democratic West, relations with Israel began a period of gradual improvement culminating with the formal establishment

of diplomatic relations in 1992. Both countries had an interest in trade with each other and in the sharing of technology,
and, as the decade of the 90s came to a close, the threat of
Islamic extremism also became a mutual concern. As we
spoke about earlier, both had limitations in natural resources
and it was Newt who was so anxious to work on green energy
with the Powers That Be in Beijing. He was very much aware
that as the 20th century had come to a close, there were new
political realities to consider. Just as there now was the major
threat of Islamic extremism, there were no longer the dual
superpowers of the United States and the Soviet Union as the
major geo-political forces. There were, however, new global
powers to contend with, foremost among them China. It was
a reality that could not be ignored, and, from a perspective of
Israel advocacy, the only question was how to best adapt. Into
this new reality came Carice Witte. She was looking to have
an impact on the China-Israel relationship in the 21st century
and founded SIGNAL to do just that.

Its mission statement reads this way, "SIGNAL, Sino-Israel
Global Network & Academic Leadership, is an action oriented
institute enhancing China's and Israel's strategic, diplomatic,
cultural, and economic relationship through high level inter-
change. SIGNAL has established significant long-term alli-
ances between China and Israel that serve as the foundation
for mutually beneficial and broad based cooperation between
the two countries." It is a frontier that Newt embraced and
Carice expressed her feeling that his support and encouragement have been critical to the success of the organization:
"Newt was unique in my life; I never had a mentor before." He
was, in fact, an important mentor for all of the grantees discussed above and many, many more. There was also another

group that he was responsible for mentoring: a new generation of philanthropists.

THE MENTOR

As much as Newt accomplished in developing organizations
and helping grantees, he realized that he could not do it alone.
Not only did that mean working with other philanthropists
from his generation, it also meant mentoring a new group of
philanthropists if the work that meant so much to him was to
continue.

Newt was introduced to Steve and Rita Emerson in 2005
when they were looking for guidance in making charitable
contributions. The Emersons were blessed with significant
resources, and, in agreement with Newt's approach to philanthropy, Newt was able to steer them to charities he felt would
best utilize their funds. He helped launch their own impressive
careers as philanthropists and they were not alone. Aubrey
and Joyce Chernick also represented the next generation of
philanthropists and they, too, were mentored by Newt. As
they recalled, "That he was with us in the world, fighting the
same battles, and pursuing the same ends, gave us hope and
courage to continue on the path he forged."

To help introduce younger and older philanthropists to
potential organizations and programs that would be worthy
of their funding, Newt created a loose network he called the
Donor Forum. It operated for about three years, was professionally staffed, and consisted of monthly meetings at which
potential grantees made presentations and requested funding
from the several dozen funders gathered at the Hillcrest Country Club to hear their pitch. It was essentially a matchmaking

service, and, though it may not have lasted, it led David Becker and Nir Boms to work on an ongoing effort to involve other foundations and funders in supporting this line of work. In January 2014, two years after Newt passed away, David and Nir felt that Newt would have been beaming when they both spoke to a group of about 50 potential, highly "qualified" funders in New York. They presented the hierarchy of impact and introduced 14 of their grantees to an appreciative audience at a summit that they helped organize.

CONTINUITY

Continuity has become a point of emphasis among many Jewish philanthropists. It is an acknowledgment that people like Newt—those who lived through the Depression, World War Two, the Holocaust, the founding of the State of Israel, and the Six Day War—were part of a unique generation. Many were children of European immigrants who were raised in big city ethnic enclaves like Glenville and Brownsville that were heavily imbued with the rich ethical and charitable legacies that characterized Eastern European Jewish life. To be able to transfer those salient values to their children and grandchildren, now largely residing in the suburbs under vastly different circumstances, would be a nearly impossible task.

It is safe to say that while Newt certainly was from a unique generation, he stood out even among exceptional people. While many other American Jews have been deeply affected by the events of the Holocaust, how many would make the prevention of another calamity their personal mission in life? While many American Jews were strong supporters of Israel, how many American Jews would devote their energies so fully, so intensely, and in so many varied and creative ways to support and strengthen the Jewish state?

Parents are often conflicted by two very different instincts. On the one hand, there is a desire to have their children follow in their footsteps, and, on the other, there is a desire for their children to develop as independent, productive, and happy people. While Newt was certainly proud and happy that Bryan had followed in his footsteps and had become a CPA, and that his daughter, Laura, a full-time mother and volunteer, had married a CPA, he expressed to me how proud he was of all of his five children: David who had earned a Ph.D. in Neuropsychology and was a scientific researcher with a university position; Daniel, who also earned a doctorate and was a composer and music professor; and Bradley, who had built from scratch his own real estate business. Whatever his own predilections, he was clearly overjoyed and very proud of their myriad accomplishments.

Just because Newt had become financially successful was no reason to spoil his five children and nine grandchildren. He did not follow the model of his peers in so many different ways such as his choice of automobile, and it is hard not to marvel at the way he discounted material things. He made it his mission, together with Rochelle, to avoid some of the pitfalls that clearly could be seen among the children of Southern California's elite. It meant limiting comforts to those that were reasonable. In this, Newt and Rochelle set an example. Just because one had the resources to build a new house and buy the latest toys did not mean it was necessary to have these things. Money was not there to be wasted. It was to be a force for good and a means to an end. Rochelle ran the family budget as if they were just a regular

Newt with four of his grandsons on the Disney Cruise (2003)

upper middle-class family. The value of a dollar was to be respected.

When flying domestically and by himself, Newt made it a habit to fly coach, eschewing on principle the temptation of flying first-class which was frequently three to four times as expensive as coach. Considered a great luxury, and a major status symbol well beyond first-class, is the private jet. Newt was an investor in some kind of private jet company and at one point a windfall developed and Newt could collect the bounty either in stock or in the use of a private jet. Needless to say, he chose the stock. He would have no part in what he considered such a decadent waste of money.

Newt imparted similar thoughts to his own children. He spoiled them little providing them with, as Rochelle put it, "enough to do something but not too much so that they would do nothing." Indeed, the nearly identical approach was made famous by Warren Buffet, the billionaire investor, who suggests in giving one's children money that the right amount is "enough so that they would feel they could do anything, but not so much that they could do nothing."

Of course, there was never any denial of the unique position that having resources bestowed on an individual. Accumulation of wealth denoted a responsibility. When Newt first asked, "What are the rich Jews doing to protect us?" he was just a boy. By the time he entered middle age, he was one of them. Newt served the Jewish Federation of Greater Los Angeles as treasurer, applying his accountant's eye and strong management skills to balancing the budget of the organization. Even after his tenure he was appointed "honorary treasurer," the first such title to be bestowed by the Federation on any individual.

The whole idea of organized Jewish social welfare—taking care of the widow, the orphan, the poor, and the struggling—has its roots within the corpus of the Torah itself. This aspect was very important for Newt to pass down. Bryan Gordon notes quite astutely that Newt's sense of helping the vulnerable was evident in his business dealings covered in previous chapters.

Another aspect of Newt's approach to money was that he never saw making money as an end it itself. And in the spirit of Jewish charitable giving, he never really saw the money that he was fortunate to make as completely his to do with as he wished. Rather he saw himself more as a guardian entrusted to do as much good and help as many people and causes as was possible. An example of this is what happened every time he had a windfall. As has been pointed out by those closest to him, the Becker Foundation came about as the result of the sale of Becker CPA Review. The sale of Electric Fuel, discussed in Chapter 6, helped establish the Becker Charitable Trust. When IBEP finally began receiving significant payments, he gave a very large sum to the Becker Foundation. That was Newt. His generosity, his strategic approach, and the way in which he conducted himself, all set a powerful example for the future generations that would carry on his work.

The legacy of providing a consistently ethical example is expressed in Hebrew as *Tocho Keboro* (the inside of the person is like the outside of the person) and was one of Newt's greatest gifts to his family. Making his children appreciate the importance of charity was another. It does not appear that he pushed them into devoting themselves to his major philanthropic and activist interests: Israel Advocacy and Defense of Democracy. Bryan was involved with Newt in this area because Newt had come to rely on his assistance in accounting and administrative matters. After 9/11, however, David became increasingly involved with the work of the Foundation, at first in his spare time. While his academic research on the neuropsychology of pain perception was very interesting and had its satisfactions, he increasingly felt that the work he was doing with Newt was very important and it came with one big plus; David could see that his philanthropic work, his effort, and his energy were having a genuine and immediate impact in very significant areas.

Eventually, Newt, at age 74, approached his oldest son and asked him to come aboard the foundation on a full-time basis as the executive director. David, at age 48, now had a decision to make. Newt Becker was known for doing things his way, and, as father and son, even in the best of situations, this can complicate things. Eventually David decided to take the risk and give it a try. A couple of years later when David's research projects concluded, he began devoting full time to philanthropy. That was in 2004, and the experiment turned out to be a great success for both parties.

One of the reasons that such arrangements often do go awry is when one party tries to fundamentally change the other. This never happened to Newt and David. Both men knew who they were and were comfortable with what they did and the way they did it. They were coming at things from different places, and, as passionate as Newt was about his positions, he developed a healthy respect for David's views. In meeting the two together as I did at AIPAC in the spring of 2011, it was evident that the chemistry and mutual admiration were both there. It was clear that Newt was very happy with the arrangement. Newt had definitely thought about the future and seemed confident that the type of work he was engaged in would continue as long as it was needed. And it was hard to imagine a speedy end to anti-Semitism, Islamic extremism, and the State of Israel facing all manner of existential threats.

Despite Newt's forward thinking and planning, it is hard to believe that he could have presaged the end coming so soon. He had health challenges to be sure; he had fought a previous battle with cancer. Years earlier, after only one chemotherapy session that Newt found unacceptably brutal he had sworn off chemotherapy. Fortunately, the cancer left his body.

His long walks, embrace of alternative medicine, and extensive vitamin regimen seemed to be paying dividends as he aged. Perhaps his energy was down, but this happens to a fair number of octogenarians, and, looking at the youthful, almost boyish grin on his face and his boundless enthusiasm for life, it was easy to forget his age. He seemed so vital, so vibrant, that if the Angel of Death ever came calling, Newt would perhaps respond to him as he did to someone he did not want to talk to on the telephone and exclaim, "I'm on another call right now, call back later."

Newt, the larger-than-life figure, the powerhouse who set out to change the world, died on January 2, 2012. It was a shock to everyone. Though he had been in and out of the hospital with an infection for over a month, everyone expected a man who knew no obstacles to bounce back as he had always done in his life. But this time things were different. Rochelle, who had called me on New Year's Eve to inform me of the terrible severity of his condition, called me again on the 2nd and asked me to prepare an obituary. Newt was laid to rest on a bright, warm day—a day of seemingly endless sunshine and bright horizons contrasted, however, by a deep gloom that was fully palpable.

There were touching eulogies at the service and afterwards as many who attended the funeral reconvened at the Hillcrest Country Club at the invitation of the family. People were allowed to give remembrances of Newt and extend condolences to the family. Bryan remembers a slew of people, this author included, coming up to tell him how sorry they felt for his loss. That is standard etiquette, but Bryan's response was most telling about the life of Newton Becker as he responded in kind, "I am sorry for *your* loss." That was the enormity of Newton D. Becker. No matter how long or how well you knew him, he left an impression on you. Without him

A Dry Bones cartoon drawn for the Becker family.

behind you, you felt a definite void. It was Bryan who realized that the loss of Newt represented much more than just the loss of a father, husband, grandfather, uncle, and friend. The loss of Newt was not restricted to the Jewish community, Los Angeles, Israel, the world of accounting or that of solar energy. As much as we have been discussing him as a Jew and as a Zionist, Newt was truly a universal figure. He did not need a bumper sticker to think globally. He had the capacity not only to change the world, but to change people. They all felt he had impacted their lives personally, professionally, intellectually, and emotionally. You could feel the collective loss from everyone assembled that very sad day.

The question was how do all of those people rebound from such a loss? For family, the loss and the burden are strongly felt every day. As this book has focused on the work that Newt so cherished, however, I will quote from David Becker's eulogy on what the future may hold. He ended his remarks with, "As Newt's successor in leading our philanthropy, I have been told by many people that I have some big shoes to fill. After reading the many tributes that have come in from all over the world the last few days, with many of them testifying to the impact that Newt's mentoring and involvement has had on their lives, it is clear to me that no one can fill his shoes. But I am proud to be his son and protégé, and with his life as a model and inspiration, Newt's legacy will continue."

In contemplating Newt and his legacy, one is reminded of the words of the great sage, Rabbi Tarfon, in *Ethics of the Fathers*: "It is not your responsibility to finish the work, but you are not free to desist from it either." No, Newt; no one can finish the work. You spent eighty-three years, significant in Jewish life because it symbolizes the average age of a man, seventy years, plus thirteen years that make up a Bar Mitzvah, laboring away and upholding the responsibility that you committed to as a boy, to do what you could to protect the Jewish people. The Jewish people owe you a debt as does Western Civilization. Now is the time, though, for others to continue the work that you so faithfully pursued. You have imparted them the requisite inspiration, wisdom, and resources to do the job. The future is in their hands, or, better put, in our hands, and the chapters of that book have yet to be written.

Newt Becker, 2009

BIBLIOGRAPHY

Berger, John J. *Charging Ahead: The Business of Renewable Energy and What it Means for America.* New York: Henry Holt & Company, 1997

Bethell, Tom. *The Longshoreman Philosopher.* Palo Alto: Hoover Institution Press, 2012

Chesnoff, Richard Z., Klein, Edward, Litell, Robert. *If Israel Lost the War.* London: Coward-McCann, 1969

Gartner, Lloyd P. *History of the Jews of Cleveland.* Cleveland: Western Reserve Historical Society, 1987

Gilder, George. *The Israel Test: Why the World's Most Besieged State is a Beacon of Freedom and Hope for the World Economy.* New York: Encounter Books, 2009

Hoffer, Eric. *The Ordeal of Change.* Titusville, New Jersey: Hopewell Publication Society, 1963

Hoffer, Eric. *The True Believer.* New York: Harper Perennial Classics, 1951

King, Thomas. *More than a Numbers Game: A Brief History of Accounting.* New York: John Wiley, 2006

Madrigal, Alex. *Powering the Dream: The History and Promise of Green Energy.* Cambridge, Massachusetts: De Capo Press, 2011

Miller, Carol Poh, Wheeler, Robert. *Cleveland: A Concise History, 1796-1996.* Bloomington: Indiana University Press, 2009

Oren, Michael. *Six Days of War: June 1967 and the Making of the Modern Middle East.* Oxford: Oxford University Press, 2002

Rubinstein, Judah, *Merging Traditions: Jewish Life in Cleveland.* Kent: Kent State University Press, 2004

Senor, Dan, Singer, Saul. *Start Up Nation: The Story of Israel's Economic Miracle.* New York: Hachette Book Group, 2009